The BUSINESS AGREEMENTS Kit

Ted Nicholas

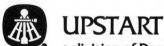

UPSTART

a division of Dearborn Publishing Group, Inc.
155 North Wacker Drive
Chicago, Illinois 60606-1719

© 1995 by Dearborn Financial Publishing, Inc.

Published by Upstart Publishing Company,
a division of Dearborn Publishing Group, Inc.

Printed in the United States of America

95 96 97 10 9 8 7 6 5 4 3 2 1

Library of Congress Cataloging-in-Publication Data

Nicholas, Ted, 1934–
    The business agreements kit / by Ted Nicholas.
        p.   cm.
    Includes index.
    ISBN 0-936894-90-3 (alk. paper)
    1. Commercial law—United States—Forms.   2. Contracts—United States—Forms.   I. Title.
    KF886.N528   1995
    346.73'07'0269—dc20
    [347.30670269]   95-13918
                                                              CIP

Books by Ted Nicholas

The Corporate Forms Kit

The Business Agreements Kit

The Complete Guide to Consulting Success (coauthor, Howard Shenson)

The Complete Guide to "S" Corporations

The Executive's Business Letter Book

43 Proven Ways To Raise Capital for Your Small Business

The Golden Mailbox: How To Get Rich Direct Marketing Your Product

How To Form Your Own Corporation Without a Lawyer for under $75.00

How To Get a Top Job in Tough Times (coauthor, Bethany Waller)

How To Get Your Own Trademark

Secrets of Entrepreneurial Leadership: Building Top Performance Through Trust and Teamwork

Contents

Chapter 3   Setting Up Your Credit and Collection Program   33

Forms

Chapter 4   Leasing Commercial Space   53

Forms

Chapter 5   The Employment Relationship   **67**

Forms

Chapter 6   Buying and Selling Goods   **97**

Forms

Chapter 7 Protecting Copyrights, Inventions, Trade Secrets and Other Intangibles **125**

Forms

Chapter 8 Assignments **133**

Forms

CHAPTER 1

How To Use Your Book

How This Book Is Designed for You

The Business Agreements Kit book/disk set was drafted for small to moderate-sized businesses. The forms we've prepared for you cover commonplace business arrangements for which you ordinarily may pay professionals. Now, you have these forms at your fingertips.

When preparing these forms, we planned to serve you in many ways:

Preventing Disputes

If you've written an agreement that spells out each person's rights, you are in the best possible position to prevent later misunderstandings caused by different recollections of just what the agreement included.

Avoiding Lawsuits

By documenting an agreement, you not only avoid disputes based on faulty memories, but you force the other party to recognize what the agreement really provides. More so than any other prevention device, a written document should stop a person who no longer likes an agreement from suing. The written agreement, he or she realizes, will keep him or her from winning any challenge based on terms other than those in the agreement.

Eliminating Legal Fees

The forms in this book can be used without paying your lawyer to pull a standard form from his or her files and charging you to fill in the blanks. More diligent lawyers will customize standard forms for their clients. Depending on your needs, you may wish to have your lawyer review these forms. However, every form in this book has been reviewed by a lawyer to ensure that it is accurate and enforceable. If you are accustomed to having your lawyer regularly prepare standard agreements for your business, *The Business Agreements Kit* can save you thousands upon thousands of dollars every year.

Ensuring Performance

We've all met a person who enters into an agreement that he or she later regrets. If the agreement is in writing, the other party knows that if he or she does not live up to the agreed-to promise, you can sue for damages. This, in turn, makes it more likely that he or she will make good on the contract's requirements.

Increasing Your Company's Efficiency

Because the forms in this book are all included on the enclosed disk, they can be copied onto your computer and used simply by filling in the blanks. You do not have to waste time and money going through the mechanical process of typing and preparing a form every time you need it.

Improving Accuracy

Again, because these forms are supplied on the enclosed disk, you avoid the possibility of a typing error that could prove costly. Remember, all you have to do is fill in the blanks.

Complying with State Laws

Many contracts must be in writing if they are to be enforceable; other contracts must follow a specific format if they are to be effective. Because the forms in this book satisfy these requirements, you can be assured that your written agreements will protect you. You may want to have an attorney review a contract to ensure that it complies with state laws.

Increasing Profits and Company Performance

By using standard forms for various business transactions, you ensure that your employees do not offer terms other than those you set as company policy. This protects your company against poor pricing and bad debts.

Avoiding Tax Difficulties

By formalizing your business agreements, you provide proof of any deductions or write-offs you take on your tax returns.

Using Forms You Can Understand

Every form is written in straightforward language that you will understand with ease. This ensures that you will not make a mistake because you did not understand the meaning of a specific provision.

Working with Your Book

Each of the chapters in this book begins with a short text section, which includes directions to guide you through the forms. That section is followed by the forms themselves.

Here is your easy-to-use guide to preparing a form:

- Start by reading the introduction to determine if there are any special instructions you must follow. The special instructions may include making duplicate copies of the form, using registered mail, having the signing of the form witnessed or notarized or using the company letterhead.
- These forms may be used as they are. Of course, new forms based on those in the book, but with changes or modifications, also can be prepared. If the form indicates that you should use your company letterhead, we've left enough room for you to copy the form on your stationery.
- Fill in all of the blanks: the date of the agreement, the names of the parties, all contract terms. If the form has provisions that you believe are not needed, just put a line through the unnecessary material and initial it (make sure the other person initials it also).
- If last-minute changes must be made to the agreement, simply write them in and have both parties initial the changes either in the margin beside the change or immediately above or below the change.
- If the signing of the agreement must be witnessed or notarized, do *not* sign it unless you are in the presence of the witness or notary public.

- If the agreement will be completed (signed) using the mail, always send two original copies to the other party and have one returned to you. If you are uncomfortable about signing the agreement before the other person signs, send an unsigned copy to the other person and have him or her return it to you. Then you can make a duplicate, sign the duplicate and return the complete agreement to the other person.
- Retain the contract for at least seven years. Even if the time during which a contract lawsuit may be brought is less than six years in your state, you should keep the contract on file for six years for tax purposes.

Signing Your Agreements

You should ensure that you sign any agreement in your true capacity. If the agreement is for a corporation, sign in your capacity as a corporate official. If you just sign your name, you can be held liable personally on the contract. If you are signing for a partnership, indicate that fact. If you are signing for yourself or your own unincorporated business, then you just have to sign your name.

Example 1: Assume that you are the president of a corporation. You should sign as follows:

ABC, Inc.
By:

_____
Robert Jones, President

Example 2: If you are signing an agreement for the benefit of a partnership, use the following format:

A&B Partnership
By:

_____
Robert Jones, Partner

Using Your Attorney

Each form was drafted by an attorney and subsequently reviewed by at least one other attorney. We are confident that these forms will serve you efficiently and safely.

The forms, however, are designed for straightforward transactions. If you are faced with a complex arrangement or one that involves large amounts of money, you would be ill-advised to try to save money by not consulting with your lawyer.

CHAPTER 2

Loans and Credit Arrangements

Introduction

This chapter contains forms designed to safeguard you as you enter into loan arrangements. As the lender, you must take measures to protect the funds you may have advanced in the form of cash or credit. This protection can come in the form of additional security, such as collateral or guaranties. Furthermore, if you are lending to a corporation, you should consider securing your loan (or credit) with the personal guaranties of the corporation's shareholders or officers. Finally, if you make a business or personal loan, a security agreement granting you an interest in property (collateral) owned by the borrower can protect your loan.

Although guaranties and collateral do protect the principal of a loan, there is one fact that you should keep in mind whenever you extend cash or credit: If you have to proceed against a guarantor or against the debtor's property, the cost of doing so will cause you to lose money. Business loans should be made only if you can be confident that the borrower will repay you without forcing you to look to guarantors or collateral.

Promissory Notes

Form 201 is designed to be used for consumer loans. It provides all of the disclosures required by the federal truth-in-lending laws. Form 202 is a promissory note that can be used when the entire loan will be repaid in one payment that will be made on a specified date. Form 203 can be used for loans that are to be repaid in either one payment or installments; it also contains a provision requiring a guaranty of payment. Form 204 is an open-ended note. It calls for payment of the amount due on demand. This form of note can be very risky for borrowers because the lender can call in the loan at any time.

Form 205 is a highly protective installment note that should be used when any significant amount of money is at issue. It contains both a guaranty and an acceleration clause. Acceleration provides that should any payment be late, then the entire amount of the note may be called. Furthermore, the note provides for attorney's fees to be paid by the borrower in the event that the lender must bring legal proceedings to collect on the note.

The guaranty supplied in Form 206 can be used in conjunction with any promissory note. It obligates the guarantor to pay in the event the note is not paid by the borrower. Keep in mind that the guaranty is only as good as the guarantor. If the guarantor is not financially sound, the promise he or she makes is essentially worthless.

Uniform Commercial Code Forms

Every state has adopted the Uniform Commercial Code (UCC); this set of laws regulates secured business transactions. The UCC governs checks, notes and transfer agreements for the sale of goods. It requires that if property is taken as collateral, the underlying security agreement or a UCC-1 (available at most stationery or office supply retail shops) must be filed with the appropriate state office and/or the county clerk of the borrower's locale. Failure to file the security agreement can cause you to lose the protection of your security interest. If you do not file, you will not have "perfected" your interest, and subsequent lenders (who would not have notice of your security interest) will have a claim to the secured property that is superior to your earlier but unfiled claim.

Another important reason to file involves the possibility that your debtor may file for bankruptcy. If you file, you are a secured creditor, and the property you have taken as security does not become available to other creditors of your debtor. If, however, you do not file and the borrower subsequently files for bankruptcy, your interest will not be protected; instead, your claim will be treated as an unsecured claim, and the property you thought would be available for your claim now will be available to all creditors.

The forms in this chapter have been designed to comply with UCC specifications. Forms 207 and 208 are pledge agreements. Form 207 can be used to take a pledge of any type of property; Form 208 should be used if the pledge involves shares of stock in a corporation (make sure the borrower has endorsed the shares in blank before you take them). Both forms differ from an ordinary security agreement in that you will be taking actual possession of the pledged collateral. Because you have actual possession of the property, no document filings are necessary.

Form 209 informs lenders who have security interests that you plan to establish a purchase money security interest as a result of a credit sale. The UCC grants you the priority in the proceeds of the sale, but only if you notify other secured parties within ten days of the sale.

Form 210 subordinates your interest to the interests of other lenders. This means that you have agreed to permit your interest to become junior to those of other creditors. Why would you make your interest inferior to the claims of others? Assume you lent money to your corporation and you've taken collateral. You may be willing to subordinate your interests to those of an outsider who is willing to lend additional money to the corporation.

Enforcing Payments

All of the forms in this section should be placed on your letterhead, either business or personal, depending on whether you made the underlying loan in your name or in the name of your business.

Form 211 states that the borrower has made full payment on the debt. Form 212 notifies the borrower that he or she is in default on the loan because of nonpayment. Form 213 should be used to notify guarantors that the note is in default and that they must honor their guaranties. With Forms 214 through 216, you can follow the three steps required by the UCC if you must execute your security agreement. Form 214 demands possession of the collateral. Forms 215 and 216 notify the debtor that the property will be put up for sale at a public (Form 215) or private (Form 216) sale.

Form 217 releases your security interest in the collateral. You should sign it when the debt has been paid and deliver it to your borrower, but only after the debt has been paid (i.e., after the payment check has cleared).

DISCLOSURE STATEMENT AND NOTE
(FEDERAL TRUTH-IN-LENDING ACT)

Date: , 19   Amount:

FOR VALUE RECEIVED, the borrower,   , residing at

                         , shall pay to the order of

         , the total amount of   dollars ($) in consecutive

payments payable on the   day of the month, beginning on   ,

19   , until the loan is paid in full.

    Failure to make a payment when due shall be a default of the loan. Should a

default exist for more than   (   ) days, the holder of this note may cause the

entire loan to be due immediately.

    1. Amount of Loan:

    2. Expenses:

    3. Total Financed:

    4. Interest Charges:

    5. Total of Payments:

    6. Annual Financed Percentage Rate:

SINGLE INSTALLMENT NOTE

FOR VALUE RECEIVED, the borrower,   , residing at
                   , who has executed this note below, shall pay to
              (the lender or his or her assignee) the principal amount of
         dollars ($), together with interest calculated at   percent
(%), per year on the outstanding balance. The entire amount, principal and
interest, shall be due and payable on or before   , 19   , at the
following address   .

    Failure to make a payment when due shall be a default of the loan. Should a
default exist for more than   (   ) days, the borrower agrees to pay the holder
of this note reasonable costs of collection including attorney's fees.

Date:_____

Borrower: _____

NOTE AND GUARANTY

FOR VALUE RECEIVED, the Borrower,   ,
residing at   , shall pay to the order of
                              (Lender), at   , the total
amount of   dollars ($), including principal and interest
at   percent (%) per year, in consecutive payments, payable on the   day
of the month beginning on   , 19   , until the loan is paid in full.
The borrower may prepay this loan without any early payment penalty.

   Failure to make a payment when due shall be a default of the loan. Should a
default exist for more than   (   ) days, the total amount outstanding may be
currently due, and the borrower agrees to pay the holder of this note reasonable
costs of collection including attorney's fees.

Date: _____

Borrower: _____

GUARANTY

   FOR VALUABLE CONSIDERATION RECEIVED, the guarantor,
                    , guarantees full payment of the above amount and shall
remain liable until the note is fully satisfied and paid in full.

Date: _____

Guarantor: _____

Address: _____

DEMAND NOTE

FOR VALUE RECEIVED, the borrower, _____ , residing at
_____ , who has executed this note below, shall pay to
_____ (the lender or his or her assignee) the principal amount of
_____ dollars ($_____), together with interest calculated at _____ percent
(_____ %) per year on the outstanding balance. The entire amount, principal and
interest, shall be due and payable ON DEMAND by holder of this note.

Failure to make a payment when due shall be a default of the loan. Should a
default exist for more than _____ (_____) days, the borrower agrees to pay the holder
of this note reasonable costs of collection including attorney's fees, as authorized
by state law.

Date: _____

Borrower: _____

PROMISSORY INSTALLMENT NOTE

Date:

THE UNDERSIGNED,   , residing at

           , jointly and severally referred to as the "Makers,"

for value received, hereby promises to pay to

(hereinafter "Payee"), the sum of   dollars ($) plus interest

at the rate of   percent (%) per annum, compounded monthly, payable in

     (   ) monthly installments of   dollars ($).

    Payments: The first payment is due on   , and monthly
payments thereafter on each and every first day of the month until the balance of
this note is fully paid. Each monthly payment is to be delivered to and payable to
the Payee, at   , either in person or by U.S. mail, and
said monthly payment must be received by the Payee prior to or on the due date of
the monthly payments.

    Default: In case of default of any monthly payment, the entire unpaid balance,
at the election of the Payee, shall become immediately due and collectible. Default
shall be defined as the Makers being more than one (1) month in arrears on the
payments due under this note.

    Confession of Judgment: Makers irrevocably authorize any attorney of any
court of record to appear for Makers at any time to waive the issuance and service
of process and to confess judgment against Makers and in favor of Payee or any
subsequent holder hereof for such amount as is unpaid with accrued interest,
together with costs and attorney's fees of thirty-three and one-third percent (33
1/3%) of the full amount due hereon (but not less than $100), and hereby ratifies
and confirms all that said attorney may do by virtue hereof, and waives and
releases all errors that may intervene in such proceedings. Venue shall lie in the
following jurisdiction:

    Collateral Security: As collateral security for the payments of this note, the
Makers will execute a Stock Pledge Agreement granting Payee a security interest
in the capital stock of   Inc., purchased from Payee this
date, and shall deliver said shares of capital stock pursuant to such Stock Pledge
Agreement.

Prepayment Option: The Makers hereby have the right to prepay the principal due on this note at any time without penalty.

_____

_____

WITNESS:

_____

GUARANTY

Date:

FOR CONSIDERATION RECEIVED, and as further incentive for _____ (hereinafter "Creditor") to advance credit to _____ residing at _____ (hereinafter "Borrower"), the undersigned (hereinafter "Guarantor") jointly and severally guarantee complete and timely payment of the liability that the Borrower owes to the Creditor. That liability is as follows:

Upon nonpayment by the Borrower of a payment properly due and owing to the Creditor, the Creditor may move against the Guarantor without the need to move first against the Borrower.

Furthermore, the Guarantor shall continue to be obligated on this guaranty until it is revoked in writing by the Creditor and the Guarantor is released by the Creditor.

This agreement shall be binding and shall attach to the successors and assigns of the Guarantor.

By: _____

    Guarantor

_____

    Address

PLEDGE

THIS AGREEMENT made this   day of   , 19   , by and
between   , husband and wife, having an address at
                          (hereinafter referred to as the "Pledgor"), and
                , whose address is
(hereinafter referred to as the "Pledgee").

WHEREAS, the Pledgor is duly indebted to the Pledgee in the aggregate
principal amount of   dollars ($), evidenced by a
promissory note of the Pledgor dated   ,19   (hereinafter
referred to as the "Note"); and

WHEREAS, in order to induce the Pledgee to loan to the Pledgor the principal
amount of the Note, the Pledgor has agreed to pledge all the following personal
property as security for the prompt payment of the Note in accordance with its
terms:

NOW, THEREFORE, intending to be legally bound hereby, the parties agree
as follows:

1. In consideration of the foregoing, the Pledgor herewith pledges, delivers
   and assigns to the Pledgee all of the above-listed property.
2. The Pledgor does hereby represent and warrant:
   (a) That, except as pledged herein, the Pledgor has not sold, assigned,
       transferred, pledged or granted any security interest in or otherwise
       hypothecated the property listed above in any manner whatsoever and
       that such property is pledged herewith free and clear of any and all
       liens, encumbrances, pledges, restrictions, security interests and
       agreements; and
   (b) That the Pledgor has the full power and authority to execute and
       deliver this pledge agreement and to pledge said property, that this
       agreement constitutes the valid and binding obligation of the Pledgor
       enforceable in accordance with its terms, and that the pledge of the

property contained herein is not in violation of any agreement, undertaking or obligation of Pledgor.

3. The Pledgee shall hold the property as security for the payment of the Note and will not at any time dispose of or encumber the same except as herein provided.

4. Upon the occurrence of an Event of Default herein defined, the Pledgee is hereby granted all of the rights and remedies accorded a secured party under the Uniform Commercial Code and may, upon ten (10) days' prior written notice to the Pledgor, sell, lease or otherwise dispose of the property pledged hereunder, at any time or from time to time, in whole or in part, at public or private sale, without advertisement or notice of sale, all of which are hereby waived, and apply the proceeds of any such sale (a) first to the expenses of holding, preparing the collateral for sale, in arranging for the sale, selling and the like, including without limitation reasonable attorney's fees and legal expenses incurred by the Pledgee (including fees and expenses of any litigation incident to any of the foregoing); (b) second to the payment of the Note and all interest accrued thereon; and (c) shall pay any excess to the Pledgor. In the event that the proceeds of any such sale are not sufficient to pay the items listed in (a) and (b) above, then the Pledgor shall remain liable and shall pay the Pledgee any such deficiency. Any purchaser at any such sale (which term shall include the Pledgee in the case of a public sale) shall receive the property free and clear of all rights of redemption or other rights or claims of the Pledgor, all of which are hereby waived.

An Event of Default hereunder is defined as:

(a) The nonpayment of any installment due and owing on the Note when it has become due;

(b) The adjudication of the Pledgor as a bankrupt or insolvent, or entry of any order, remaining unstayed by appeal or otherwise for twenty (20) days, appointing a receiver or trustee for the Pledgor or for all or any of the Pledgor's properties, or the filing by or against the Pledgor of a petition seeking any of the foregoing or consenting thereto, or the filing of a petition to take advantage of any debtors' act, or making a general assignment for the benefit of creditors or admitting in writing the inability to pay debts as they may mature.

5. This is the entire agreement between the parties hereto and may be changed only by a written instrument signed by the party against whom any charge is sought to be enforced.

6. This agreement is made in and shall be governed by and construed in accordance with the laws of the state of   .

7. This agreement shall be binding upon and inure to the benefit of the parties hereto, their respective heirs, personal representatives, successors and assigns.

IN WITNESS WHEREOF, the Pledgor, intending to be legally bound hereby has executed this agreement the day and year first above written.

_____

_____

WITNESS:

_____

STOCK PLEDGE

THIS AGREEMENT made this   day of   , 19   , by and between   , husband and wife, having an address at   (hereinafter referred to as the "Pledgor"), and   , whose address is (hereinafter referred to as the "Pledgee"). WITNESSETH:

WHEREAS, the Pledgor is duly indebted to the Pledgee in the aggregate principal amount of   dollars ($) evidenced by a promissory note of the Pledgor dated   , 19   (hereinafter referred to as the "Note"); and

WHEREAS, to induce the Pledgee to loan to the Pledgor the principal amount of the Note, the Pledgor has agreed to pledge all of their shares of   , Inc., as security for the prompt payment of the Note in accordance with its terms.

NOW, THEREFORE, intending to be legally bound hereby, the parties agree as follows:

1. In consideration of the foregoing, the Pledgor herewith pledges, delivers and assigns to the Pledgee all of their shares of   , Inc., duly endorsed in blank, and does hereby appoint the Pledgee, or its nominee, the Pledgor's true and lawful attorney and in its name, place and stead to cause the shares of   , Inc., to be transferred on the books of the corporation to the name of the Pledgee.

2. The Pledgor does hereby represent and warrant:

   (a) That, except as pledged herein, the Pledgor has not sold, assigned, transferred, pledged or granted any security interest in or otherwise hypothecated the shares of stock of   , Inc., in any manner whatsoever and that the shares of stock of   , Inc., are pledged herewith free and clear of any and all liens, encumbrances, pledges, restrictions, security interests and agreements; and

   (b) That the Pledgor has full power and authority to execute and deliver this pledge agreement and to pledge the shares of stock of   , Inc., hereunder, that this agreement constitutes the valid and binding obligation of the Pledgor enforceable in accordance with its terms, and that the pledge of the shares of stock of   , Inc., contained herein, is not in violation of any agreement, undertaking or obligation of the Pledgor.

3. The Pledgee shall hold the shares of stock of   , Inc., as security for the payment of the Note and will not at any time dispose of or encumber the same except as herein provided. Although the Pledgee is the holder of the shares of stock of   , Inc., it shall not collect dividends thereon and the Pledgor shall have the right to cast any vote of the same at meetings of stockholders of the corporation, at which said stock may be entitled to vote so long as an Event of Default, herein set forth, has not occurred and, if the Pledgee has exercised its right to have the shares of stock of   , Inc., in its name as aforesaid, the Pledgee agrees to execute any and all proxies in favor of the Pledgor that may be required. Upon the payment of the Note in full, the Pledgee shall retransfer or redeliver the shares of stock of   , Inc., to the Pledgor.

4. Upon the occurrence of an Event of Default herein defined, the Pledgee is hereby granted all of the rights and remedies accorded a secured party under the Uniform Commercial Code and may, upon ten (10) days prior written notice to the Pledgor, sell, lease or otherwise dispose of the shares of stock of   , Inc., pledged hereunder, at any time or from time to time, in whole or in part, at public or private sale, without advertisement or notice of sale, all of which are hereby waived, and apply the proceeds of any such sale (a) first to the expenses of holding, preparing the collateral for sale, in arranging for the sale, selling and the like, including without limitation reasonable attorney's fees and legal expenses incurred by the Pledgee (including fees and expenses of any litigation incident to any of the foregoing); (b) second to the payment of the Note and all interest accrued thereon; and (c) shall pay any excess to the Pledgor.

In the event that the proceeds of any such sale are not sufficient to pay the items listed in (a) and (b) above, then the Pledgor shall remain liable and shall pay the Pledgee any such deficiency. Any purchaser at any such sale (which term shall include the Pledgee in the case of a public sale) shall receive the shares of stock of _____, Inc., free and clear of all rights of redemption or other rights or claims of the Pledgor, all of which are hereby waived.

An Event of Default hereunder is defined as:

(a) The nonpayment of any installment due and owing on the Note when it has become due;

(b) The adjudication of the Pledgor as a bankrupt or insolvent, or entry of any order, remaining unstayed by appeal or otherwise for twenty (20) days, appointing a receiver or trustee for the Pledgor or for all or any of the Pledgor's properties, or the filing by or against the Pledgor of a petition seeking any of the foregoing or consenting thereto, or the filing of a petition to take advantage of any debtors' act, or making a general assignment for the benefit of creditors or admitting in writing inability to pay debts as they may mature.

5. This is the entire agreement between the parties hereto and may be changed only by a written instrument signed by the party against whom any charge is sought to be enforced.

6. This agreement is made in and shall be governed by and construed in accordance with the laws of the state of _____.

7. This agreement shall be binding upon and inure to the benefit of the parties hereto, their respective heirs, personal representatives, successors and assigns.

IN WITNESS WHEREOF, the Pledgor, intending to be legally bound hereby, has executed this agreement the day and year first above written.

_____

_____

WITNESS:

_____

NOTICE TO SECURED PARTY
OF PURCHASE MONEY SECURITY INTEREST

Date:

To:

Dear   :

Please be advised that we have or will shortly have a purchase money security interest in the following secured collateral:

The property listed above will be sold to:

to satisfy our claim.

We are providing this notice to you, as a holder of a security interest, of our claim of priority in the collateral.

Sincerely,

_____

SUBORDINATION AGREEMENT (FULL)

FOR VALUABLE CONSIDERATION, receipt of which is acknowledged,
                              (Creditor), the beneficiary of a security interest granted
by   (Debtor), dated   , 19   , hereby
agrees to subordinate to   (Senior Creditor) the Creditor's
security interest against the Debtor up to the following amount:
dollars ($).
Signed this   day of   , 19   .
Creditor: _____
Agreed to:
Debtor: _____

RECEIPT ACKNOWLEDGING PAYMENT IN FULL

RECEIPT of   dollars ($) is accepted as complete payment
in satisfaction of the outstanding claim from   , the
Debtor, for the following obligation:

Signed this   day of   , 19   .
Creditor: _____

NOTICE OF PROMISSORY NOTE DEFAULT

Date:

To:

PURSUANT to the terms of a certain promissory note dated   ,
19   , you have failed to make the required payment. Failure to pay constitutes
a default of the note.

PURSUANT to the note, the entire amount, including interest,
dollars ($), is now due and payable.

Should you not correct the default or pay the entire outstanding amount
within   (   ) days from the date of this letter, this matter will be forwarded
to our counsel for appropriate collection actions.

Sincerely,

_____

NOTICE TO GUARANTOR OF DEFAULT ON NOTE

Date:

To:

PURSUANT to the terms of a certain promissory note dated   ,
19   , the borrower has failed to make the required payment. Failure to pay
constitutes a default of the note.

PURSUANT to the note, the entire amount, including interest,
dollars ($) is now due and payable.

You are the guarantor of the note. Should you not pay the entire outstanding
amount in the following   (   ) days, this matter will be forwarded for
appropriate collection actions.

Sincerely,

_____

SECURED PARTY'S DEMAND FOR COLLATERAL

Date:

To:

PURSUANT to the terms of a certain security agreement and promissory note dated   , 19   , you are in default due to your failure to:

　　Therefore, you must turn over the collateral to my representative pursuant to the security agreement and the Uniform Commercial Code.

　　　　　　　　　　Sincerely,

　　　　　　　　　　_____

PUBLIC SALE NOTICE

Date:

To:

PURSUANT to the terms of a certain security agreement and promissory note
dated   , 19   , you are hereby notified that the property held
as collateral will be sold at an auction open to the public. The date, time and place
of the auction are:

Date:

Time:

Place:

In the event that the sale of the collateral at the auction does not provide
sufficient funds to satisfy the underlying debt, you will continue to be responsible
for any remaining deficiency.

Your property may be reclaimed by paying the entire amount due before the
sale.

Sincerely,

_____

PRIVATE SALE NOTICE

Date:

To:

PURSUANT to the terms of a certain security agreement and promissory note dated _____ , 19 _____ , you are hereby notified that the property held as collateral under the security agreement and promissory note will be sold at a private sale on _____ , 19 _____ .

    The property to be sold at the private sale consists of:

    The private buyer shall be _____ .

    You will continue to be responsible for any deficiency if the proceeds of the sale are insufficient to satisfy the full amount of your debt.

    Your property may be reclaimed by paying the entire amount due before the sale.

                    Sincerely,

                    _____

SECURITY INTEREST RELEASE

FOR VALUABLE CONSIDERATION RECEIVED, the secured party releases the lien created by a certain security interest, dated   , 19   , granted by   (debtor) to   , the secured party.

      This release is a complete release of all liens created by the above-noted security interest.

Dated: _____

_____
Secured Party

CHAPTER 3

Setting Up Your Credit and Collection Program

Introduction

The current business environment demands that every business establish a credit and collection program. This chapter provides you with forms you will need to minimize the impact of bad-debt write-offs. The forms address the three functions of a credit and collection program: granting credit, monitoring your credit accounts and collecting outstanding accounts in a timely fashion.

Granting Credit

Federal lending laws limit what you may ask of a consumer borrower. Form 301 satisfies the federal government's requirement. Form 302 can be used for your business customers.

In the event that you are seeking credit and an incorrect, unfavorable credit report has been made, the Fair Credit Reporting Act provides you with a right to correct any errors and to demand that a copy of your request be attached to any report that the credit reporting agency issues to its clients. Form 303 asserts your rights under the Fair Credit Reporting Act.

If you opt to reject a credit application, Form 304 can be used to explain your decision to the applicant. Form 305 informs a customer that he or she has exceeded his or her credit limit and advises the customer that payment must accompany any future orders or that you will ship future orders cash on delivery (COD). You may wish to modify this form for use when a customer is approaching his or her credit limit.

Monitoring Processes

Form 306 provides a formal structure for your company's receivables department to report the status of accounts. Your company's internal procedures should require the person who prepares the report to sign it. The form also requires the person preparing the report to recommend a future course of action with respect to the customer named in the report. The credit manager's recommendations should be reviewed and acted on.

Forms 307 through 312 should be on business letterhead stationery. Form 307 is a friendly note designed to make your customer come forward. At this point, you can assume that you may be able to work out an arrangement that will not injure the business relationship that you have with your customer.

Forms 308 and 309 are follow-up notices that should be used if you have not received a response to Form 307. Form 309 should be sent by certified mail with a return receipt requested.

If the customer's response to any of these form letters is to suggest installment payments of the outstanding balance on his or her account, Form 310 should be used to memorialize any agreement that you may have worked out with the customer. Remember, this form is a contract between you and your debtor. You must send a signed original and a signed copy of the letter agreement to the customer and require him or her to return a signed copy to you. In other words, both copies should be signed as originals.

If all other efforts have failed, then you should forward your collection problem (include copies of unpaid invoices and your collection letters) to your attorney or collection agency. Form 311 can be used for this purpose. Form 312 should be used to ensure that your lawyer or collection agency keeps your account at the top of its work list. Remember, attorneys and collection agencies work for you; do not be shy about asking for updates. Form 313 can be an important weapon if you will have to sue to collect the debt. In this form, the customer admits that he or she owes you money. If used early in the collection process, the customer may be willing to sign it to stay in your good graces. If it eventually becomes necessary to sue, the customer's admission of the debt in Form 313 can prevent him or her from challenging the legitimacy of your claim.

Payment Forms

Form 314 should be used to acknowledge cash payment from a customer. Form 315 notifies your customer that a check he or she gave you was not honored by the bank. Before using Form 315, you should call your local law enforcement authorities, either the police department or the county prosecutor's office. In many states, writing a bad check is a crime.

CONSUMER CREDIT APPLICATION

Name: Social Security #:

Street:

City: State: Zip Code:

Telephone:

Employer: Supervisor:

Employer's Address: Telephone:

Annual Salary: Years Employed:

Position:

Additional Income:

Personal:

Date of Birth: Dependents:

Home: Owned   Rented   Live with parents

Mortgage holder or Landlord: Monthly Payment:

Credit Sources:

Did you ever declare bankruptcy or have a judgment filed against you?

If yes, list the court and date:

Bank:

    Checking Account:

    Savings Account:

    Bank Address:

Credit Cards (list account number, balance and monthly payment):

    Visa:

    Mastercard:

    American Express:

    Diners Club:

    Discover:

SIGNATURE (ALL APPLICANTS)

The information contained in this application is true and complete, and is supplied to obtain credit from you. I authorize you to verify any and every aspect of the information in the application and any additional information that you may require in connection with this application or in connection with any review, update, extension, renewal or collection of any credit you extend as a result of this application. I also authorize you to report your credit experience with me to others such as banks, retail establishments and credit-reporting agencies.

KEEPING APPLICATION: The undersigned agrees that this application may be retained whether or not you approve it.

ACKNOWLEDGMENT: The undersigned acknowledges receipt of a Notice Regarding Credit Reports.

Applicant 1 Signature: _____ Date: _____

Applicant 2 Signature: _____ Date: _____

CREDIT APPLICATION FOR A BUSINESS

Name of Business:

Type of Business: General Partnership   Corporation

                   Limited Partnership   Sole Proprietorship

Address:

Federal ID# or Social Security #:

Partners/Owner/President:

Address:

Telephone: (Home)   (Business)

Date Business Started:

Dun and Bradstreet Rating:

Amount of Credit Requested:

Bank: Account #:

Credit References:

Trade References:

     Are you a defendant in a lawsuit? Yes No (Circle one.) If so, list and describe the lawsuits:

     The undersigned agrees to the release of its credit history. We understand that if credit is extended, it may be canceled without notice.

_____

NOTICE CORRECTING CREDIT INFORMATION

Date:

To:

Gentlemen/Mesdames:

It has come to my attention that the following negative information is listed on my credit history:

These data are incorrect in the following aspects:

Pursuant to the Fair Credit Reporting Act, I ask that this letter be attached to my credit history and that it be included with any response that your company makes to any and all credit requests made on my account.

Kindly receipt and return the enclosed copy of this letter.

Your prompt cooperation is greatly appreciated.

Sincerely,

_____

Social Security #: _____

EXPLANATION OF CREDIT REJECTION

Date:

To:

On   , 19   , you requested an explanation of why your application for credit was refused. Our reasons for declining to extend credit to you are based on the following information that we received:

We appreciate your past patronage and welcome your future patronage; if you believe the above information is incorrect in any fashion, please do not hesitate to write to us at your convenience.

Sincerely,

_____

CREDIT LIMIT NOTIFICATION

Date:

To:

Reviewing your account, we have noted that you have a current outstanding account balance of   dollars (\$). Your account limit has been set at   dollars (\$).

    You are currently in excess of your account limitation. Your business is important to us; however, until you reduce your outstanding account balance, future orders will be shipped either prepaid or cash on delivery (COD).

    If you believe your situation justifies an increase in your account limit, we would be pleased to discuss it with you.

                      Sincerely,

_____

ACCOUNTS RECEIVABLE REPORT

Client:

Client Number:

Address:

Receivables analysis:

Less than 30 days:

30 to 60 days:

61 to 90 days:

Over 90 days:

Total outstanding:

Payment agreement with client: Yes No (Circle one.) If a payment agreement exists, set out the terms:

If no payment agreement exists, circle one of the recommended actions listed below:

Continue to ship

Require payment plan

Ship cash on delivery (COD)

Turn over for collection action

_____

Accounts Receivable Department

OVERDUE NOTICE

Date:

To:

Have you forgotten us? Our bill, dated   , 19   , was due on
                    , 19   . If you have mailed your payment, please disregard
this notice and accept our sincere thanks.

    If not, please mail your check in the amount of   dollars
($) today.

    Thank you.

                       Sincerely,

_____

SECOND OVERDUE PAYMENT NOTICE

Date:

To:

Dear   :

We wrote to you about your past due bill on   , 19   . We have not as of yet received payment.

    If you have mailed your payment, please disregard this notice and accept our sincere thanks. If not, please mail your check in the amount of dollars ($) today.

    If we do not receive payment within ten (10) working days of the date of this letter, we shall be obliged to take appropriate action to enforce our rights.

    Thank you.

Sincerely,

_____

FINAL OVERDUE NOTICE

Date:

To:

Dear   :

We wrote to you on   , 19   , and again on   ,
19   , about your past due bill in the amount of   dollars
($).

  We have not as of yet received payment. If we do not receive payment within
seven (7) business days, we will be forced to turn your account over to a
collection agency. Such action may impact your credit history in an unfavorable
fashion.

  If you have mailed your payment, please disregard this notice and accept our
sincere thanks.

Sincerely,

_____

INSTALLMENT ACCOUNT SETTLEMENT

Date:

To:

Dear   :

We are pleased to settle your outstanding receivable by agreeing to an installment plan whereby you will pay off the outstanding balance in installments of
_____ dollars ($_____) per _____. Under this agreement, your first payment will be due on _____,19 .

    We look forward to your future business. If this meets with your understanding, kindly sign the enclosed copy of this letter agreement under the words "Agreed to and accepted" and return that signed copy to us.

    Thank you.

Sincerely,

_____

Agreed to and accepted:

_____

COLLECTION DISPATCH

Date:

To:

Dear   :

Enclosed are the following outstanding accounts. Kindly begin the appropriate collection proceedings.

Customer   Invoice Number   Outstanding Balance

   Please advise of any and all actions that you take with respect to the above accounts receivable.

Sincerely,

_____

COLLECTION EFFORTS UPDATE

Date:

To:

Kindly report on your efforts regarding the following accounts that we transmitted
to your office in a letter dated   , 19   :

Customer   Invoice Number   Outstanding Balance

Sincerely,

_____

ACKNOWLEDGMENT OF ACCOUNT BALANCE

Date:

The undersigned agrees that he or she owes to   the
amount of   dollars ($). Furthermore, I agree that there are
no credits or setoffs that have not been reflected in my account.

_____
Customer

RECEIPT

Receipt of _____ dollars ($ _____) is hereby acknowledged. Said amount was paid in (circle one): cash check number: _____ .

Date: _____

_____

OVERDRAFT CHECK NOTICE

Date:

To:

Dear   :

Your check number   , in the amount of   dollars ($)
has been returned by your bank as uncollectible funds. You must make this check
good within   (   ) days. Should we not receive such funds promptly, we
shall pursue all appropriate legal actions.

_____

CHAPTER 4

Leasing Commercial Space

Introduction

This chapter provides the forms necessary for simple landlord-tenant situations. In the relatively uncomplicated lease transaction, the parties themselves can satisfy their needs using the forms in this chapter. More complicated lease arrangements, however, should be drafted by a professional because the variables are so great that even the smallest error can prove far more costly than the fee that your attorney will charge for his or her efforts.

Leases

Form 401 sets out a simple lease that is useful in most business situations. Form 402 documents any lease revisions agreed to by both the landlord and the tenant. In the event that the landlord and the tenant agree to extend the lease beyond its expiration date, Form 403 can be used to document that agreement.

Form 404 permits one tenant to transfer (assign) his or her rights under a lease to another tenant. Before entering into such an agreement (whether you are assigning or taking an assignment), examine the lease to ensure that it can be assigned. You will note that the form also calls for the landlord to sign the assignment—this anticipates and avoids any possibility that the landlord will object to the new tenant.

If the landlord and the tenant agree to terminate a lease, Form 405 documents that agreement and protects both parties from any subsequent disagreement on the question of whether there was such an agreement.

Fixtures and Lease Terminations

Form 406 protects the tenant's right to fixtures that he or she may have installed on the leased property. Local property law may grant title to the landlord for fixtures installed. This form establishes the tenant's rights to such property. If you are a tenant and you intend to improve the property that you are renting, you should use this form. One of the most frequently litigated issues involving landlords and tenants involves the question of who owns the improvements made by the tenants.

Form 407, which should be on the tenant's business stationery, provides the landlord with notice that the tenant is ending an at-will tenancy. A prudent tenant will either ask the landlord to return a signed copy of the form or send the notice by certified mail with a return receipt requested.

Form 408 can be used by the landlord to demand that the tenant vacate the premises based on the tenant's failure to pay rent. Note that the form demands that the tenant leave the rented property in broom-clean condition. Prudent landlords send this form by certified mail and request a return receipt in order to avoid any claim by the tenant that the landlord acted without notice.

Form 409 should be used by a landlord to provide notice to the tenant that an at-will tenancy will terminate. Although not required by most state laws, this notice should be sent by certified mail with a return receipt requested.

LEASE AGREEMENT

LEASE AGREEMENT made this   day of   , 19   , between
                    , with an address at
(hereinafter referred to as "Landlord") and   , with an
address at   (hereinafter referred to as "Tenant").

It is therefore agreed:

1. Premises: The Landlord shall lease to the Tenant the premises
   located at:

2. Lease Term: The term of this lease shall be for a period of   (   )
   year(s), commencing   , 19   , and terminating
                   , 19   . The lease term can be extended only by
   mutual agreement of the parties hereto.

3. Rental Amount: The Tenant shall pay to the Landlord an annual sum of
            dollars ($) to lease the property. Rental
   payments shall be made in monthly payments, each of which shall be in
   the amount of   dollars ($), and each of which
   shall be paid on the   day of the month.

4. Option To Renew: The Tenant shall have an option to renew this lease on
   the premises for a   (   )-year period upon the following terms and
   conditions: The Tenant's option to renew must be exercised in writing
   and must be received by the Landlord no less than   (   ) days
   before the expiration of this lease or any extensions thereof.

5. Arbitration: Any controversy or claim arising out of or relating to this
   lease agreement or the breach thereof shall be settled by arbitration in
   accordance with the rules then obtaining of the American Arbitration
   Association, and judgment upon the award rendered may be entered and
   enforced in any court having jurisdiction thereof.

6. No Violation or Breach: The Landlord and the Tenant warrant and
   represent each to the other that the performance of this agreement does
   not violate any laws, statutes, local ordinances or state or federal
   regulations regarding controlled substances, or otherwise, or any court
   order or administrative order or ruling, nor is such performance in

violation of any loan document's conditions or restrictions in effect for financing, whether secured or unsecured.

7. Benefit: This agreement shall be binding upon and inure to the benefit of the parties hereto and their legal representatives, successors and assigns.

8. Notices: Any notice required or desired to be given under this agreement shall be deemed given if in writing sent by certified mail to the addresses of the parties to this lease agreement as follows:

    Landlord:

    Tenant:

9. Captions: Captions are used in this agreement for convenience only and are not intended to be used in the construction or in the interpretation of this agreement.

10. Invalid Provision: In the event any provision of this agreement is held to be void, invalid or unenforceable in any respect, then the same shall not affect the remaining provisions hereof, which shall continue in full force and effect.

11. Entire Agreement: This agreement contains the entire understanding of the parties. It may not be changed orally. This agreement may be amended or modified only in writing that has been executed by both parties hereto.

12. Interpretation: This lease agreement shall be interpreted under the laws of the state of   .

                                Landlord

                                By:

                                _____

                                _____

                                Tenant

LEASE AMENDMENT

FOR CONSIDERATION MUTUALLY EXCHANGED between the parties,
(hereinafter "Landlord") and
(hereinafter "Tenant"), this lease amendment is made this   day of   ,
19   .

    WHEREAS, the Landlord and the Tenant have previously entered into a lease
agreement dated   , 19   ; and

    WHEREAS, both parties desire to amend the lease;

    NOW, therefore, intending to be legally bound, both parties agree as follows:

    In all other respects, said lease shall continue in full force and effect.

    IN WITNESS WHEREOF, the parties have executed this lease amendment the
day and year first above written.

                    Landlord

                    By:

_____

_____

                    Tenant

LEASE EXTENSION

FOR CONSIDERATION MUTUALLY EXCHANGED between the parties,
                    (hereinafter "Landlord") and
(hereinafter "Tenant"), this extension agreement is made this   day of
      , 19   .

    WHEREAS, the Landlord and the Tenant previously entered into a lease
dated   , 19   ; and

    WHEREAS, said agreement will conclude on   , 19   ; and

    WHEREAS, both parties desire to extend the lease;

    NOW, therefore intending to be legally bound, both parties agree:

1. The agreement shall be lengthened for an additional term of

2. During the duration of this extension, the monthly rent shall be in the
    amount of   dollars ($).

3. In all other respects, said lease shall continue in full force and effect.

    IN WITNESS WHEREOF, the parties have executed this agreement the day
and year first above written.

                      Landlord

                      By:

                      _____

                      _____

                      Tenant

LEASE ASSIGNMENT AGREEMENT

AGREEMENT entered into this   day of   , 19   , by and
between   (hereinafter "Assignor") and
                               (hereinafter "Assignee") and
(hereinafter "Landlord").

WHEREAS, the Assignor is the tenant of leased premises located at
                              ; and

WHEREAS, the Assignor desires to assign said lease rights to
                              ; and

WHEREAS, the Assignee desires to acquire said lease.

NOW, THEREFORE, for good and valuable consideration, the parties hereto
agree as follows:

1. <u>Sale of Lease.</u> The Assignor shall assign it rights in the above-mentioned lease to the Assignee. The lease representing said leasehold interest is attached hereto and made a part hereof as Exhibit "A."

2. <u>Purchase Price.</u> The purchase price for the sale of the lease rights as described in paragraph 1 above shall be   dollars ($). The Assignee shall tender to the Landlord a check in the amount of   dollars ($).

3. <u>Date the Assignor Shall Vacate the Leased Premises.</u> The Assignor shall vacate the leased premises no later than   , 19   . The Assignor may vacate the leased premises prior to   , 19   , provided that the Assignor notifies the Landlord and the Assignee of such occurrence at least   (   ) weeks prior to the date of vacating. The leased premises shall be left in broom-clean condition, and the Assignor shall, prior to the date of vacating, remove from the leased premises all items of personalty belonging to the Assignor.

4. <u>Proration of Rent.</u> The Assignee hereby agrees to reimburse the Assignor for all rents paid by the Assignor to the Landlord that represent rental payments for the period of time after the date of vacating by the Assignor.

5. Waiver of Breach. The waiver by any party to this agreement of a breach of any provision of this agreement by any party shall not operate or be construed as a waiver of any subsequent breach by any party. No waiver shall be valid unless in writing and signed by the parties to this agreement.

6. Captions. Captions are used in this agreement for convenience only and are not intended to be used in the construction or in the interpretation of this agreement.

7. Interpretation. This agreement shall be interpreted in accordance with the laws of the state of   .

8. Enforceability. In the event that any provision of this agreement is held to be void, invalid or unenforceable in any respect, then the same shall not affect the remaining provisions or subprovisions hereof, which shall continue in full force and effect.

9. Binding Effect. This agreement shall bind the parties hereto, their legal representatives, successors and assigns. The Assignee assumes and undertakes all of the terms and conditions of the lease as its own obligations.

10. Entire Agreement. This agreement contains the entire understanding of the parties. It may not be changed orally. This agreement may be amended or modified only with such writing being executed by the parties hereto.

IN WITNESS WHEREOF, the parties have caused this agreement to be executed on the date first above written.

Landlord

By:

_____

Assignor

By:

_____

Assignee

By:

_____

AGREED LEASE TERMINATION

FOR CONSIDERATION MUTUALLY EXCHANGED between the parties, and , this agreement is made this day of , 19 .

WHEREAS, and previously entered into a lease dated , 19 ; and

WHEREAS, both parties desire to terminate the lease;

NOW, THEREFORE, intending to be legally bound, both parties agree as follows:

1. Said lease shall cease as of , 19 .

2. Both parties agree to release each other of all liability under the lease, except for such obligations that arose prior to the cancellation date set out in paragraph 1 above.

3. In all other respects, said agreement shall continue in full force and effect.

IN WITNESS WHEREOF, the parties have executed this agreement the day and year first above written.

_____
Landlord

_____
Tenant

WITNESS:

_____

LANDLORD'S WAIVER OF CLAIM TO FIXTURES

FOR VALUABLE CONSIDERATION, receipt of which is acknowledged, _____ (hereinafter "Landlord") hereby surrenders any claim to personal property that has been affixed to the real property located at _____ and leased by _____ (hereinafter "Tenant") under a lease dated _____, 19___, a copy of which is attached hereto. Furthermore, the Landlord also surrenders any claim to any personal property installed on the property by the Tenant, even if such property may be deemed to be a fixture upon the property.

    The Landlord acknowledges and admits that said fixtures retain their status of personal property and may be removed by the Tenant.

Dated: _____

_____
Landlord

_____
Tenant

TENANT'S NOTICE ENDING AT-WILL TENANCY

Date:

To:

Dear   :

I am your tenant-at-will in your property located at:

By means of this letter, you are hereby informed that the tenancy will end on
                    , 19   , and that the premises will be vacated on or before that
date.

Please acknowledge your receipt of this notice by returning the enclosed copy
of this letter to the undersigned at the address shown above.

Sincerely,

_____

Tenant

Receipt Acknowledged:

_____

Landlord

NOTICE TO VACATE FOR FAILURE TO PAY RENT

Date:

To:

Dear   :

You are the tenant of premises located at   and
occupy the premises under a lease dated   , 19   .

The above-mentioned lease calls on you to make monthly rental payments of
dollars ($). You are now in arrears in the amount of
dollars ($), having failed and refused to pay your rent
since   , 19   , as you are obligated to do under the terms of the
above-mentioned lease.

Accordingly, you are required to pay the above sum within three (3) days after
you receive this notice or surrender possession of the premises in a broom-clean
condition to the Landlord. Your failure to comply will result in the Landlord
commencing eviction proceedings under the statute to recover possession of the
premises.

Sincerely,

_____

Landlord

By:

_____

LANDLORD'S NOTICE ENDING AT-WILL TENANCY

Date:

To:

Dear   :

You are the tenant occupying the property located at   ,
under the terms of a lease dated   , 19   .

    Your tenancy under that lease is a tenancy at will. You are hereby advised that
your tenancy shall end on   , 19   , and you are hereby directed
to vacate the leased premises no later than that date.

    We also remind you that under the terms of the lease, you are required to
leave the premises in broom-clean condition.

                   Sincerely,

_____

                   Landlord

CHAPTER 5

The Employment Relationship

Introduction

This chapter provides forms designed to safeguard your business in its employment practices, starting with an employee's hiring until the time he or she leaves your employ. Essentially, the forms address ordinary work relationships. As a practical matter, they cannot address specific federal laws that can affect the employment relationship. For example, despite the existence of a valid contract, your company still must satisfy many state and federal laws bearing on the employment relationship. For instance, an employee who is covered by minimum wage laws cannot waive his or her right to that minimum wage, even if an otherwise valid contract provides for a lower pay scale.

Similarly, an employment contract cannot waive an employee's right to be free of discriminatory treatment on the job. Keep in mind that federal and state antidiscrimination laws cover employees who are treated unfairly because of age, race, national origin, physical handicap, religion or sex. Furthermore, the reach of these laws—at both the state and federal levels—is very long. The case books are filled with litigation involving relatively small firms that have been forced to rehire former employees at higher levels and even provide back pay for a year or more that the employees were not on the payroll.

Initial Employment

Form 501 should be written on your company's stationery. It is directed to a job applicant's former employer and asks for references. Do not be surprised if the response is limited to an acknowledgment that the individual was employed during a certain time period. Many employers are unwilling to respond more fully because they fear that their former employees might sue them if references contain anything that might be construed as unfavorable, even if the references are completely truthful. If your written requests do not yield more than a list of previous employment dates, you may wish to consider telephoning prior employers. One simple way to get around their reluctance to answer specific questions is to ask whether the former employees are qualified to be rehired by their companies. If the answer is no, you may want to reconsider the applicant's potential for your company.

Form 502 is an in-house evaluation format that you should adopt to ensure that all job applicants go through the same process and that every aspect of your hiring process (including credential checking) is followed.

If your company requires job applicants to undergo a medical examination, you must protect yourself by keeping a written consent from each applicant in your permanent files. Form 503 is designed for just this purpose.

Form 504 provides a simple, letter-format employment contract for employment at will. An at-will employee is one who can quit at any time and who can be fired at any time. Many states still recognize that employment without a contract is an at-will relationship. There is a growing trend in some courts, however, to hold that employees who do not have a written agreement and who have long-term tenure cannot be fired at the employer's will. Form 504 confirms the at-will nature of the relationship and strengthens the employer's position when a long-term, at-will employee is fired.

Caveat: Even if an employment contract states an employee is hired at will, many courts nevertheless will incorporate the provisions of your employee handbook (or other rules published by the employer) into the at-will contract. If your employee handbook provides that an employee cannot be fired unless a specified procedure is followed, then the courts may well conclude that you cannot fire the employee at your will, but that you must follow the procedures set out in the handbook.

Form 505 is a formal employment contract for a salesperson. It contains a promise that obligates the employee not to compete with the employer after he or she leaves the company's employ. This is an employer-oriented form and many of its provisions provide additional levels of protection for the employer. Read it carefully and implement those most useful to you.

Form 506 protects the employer in the event the Internal Revenue Service disallows a payment that reimburses an employee for business expenses. It is used most often as part of an employment agreement (either standing alone or as part of the employment contract) with officers/owners and protects the employer from adverse tax treatment. Form 507 is an expense account report form. It provides a structure with which an employee can be reimbursed and will help you treat those expenses correctly for tax purposes.

Form 508 protects the employer when an agency, such as a mortgage company, bank or credit-card company, requests information about an employee. You should have the employee sign this form before you release information to protect you in the event that a disgruntled employee should seek to sue for invasion of privacy.

Noncompetition Agreements

.Form 509 prohibits employees from taking clients when they leave your employ. This form suggests that you have the agreement notarized. Although notarization is not required by law, it does drive home to the employee how seriously you take the noncompetition agreement and will do away with any potential claim by the employee that he or she does not recall signing such an agreement.

If they are to be upheld by the courts, noncompetition agreements must be "reasonable" as to both duration and area covered. They should not be so overly burdensome as to appear punitive. Essentially, the agreement should do no more than protect your current and reasonable future needs. For example, if your company does business throughout a 50-mile radius and you have begun plans to expand so that you can serve a 100-mile area, the noncompetition agreement should seek to protect you within a 100-, not a 50-mile radius.

With respect to the duration of a noncompetition agreement, it is clear from existing precedent that most courts will enforce agreements that restrict employees for up to one year after they leave their jobs. If the restriction lasts for a longer term, most courts will require the employers to demonstrate that the time periods are reasonable.

Terminating Employees

Forms 510, 511 and 512 have taken on increased importance in today's legal environment. Properly documenting an employee's personnel file is an absolute necessity if you want to fire an individual today. A host of federal laws, including the Equal Employment Opportunity Act and the Age Discrimination in Employment Act, grant the disgruntled employee recourse for improper termination.

The three forms provided in this section provide a format that you should follow both in form and in spirit. First, meet with the employee whose work is not up to par and explain what the problem is and how you expect the employee to correct it. Then, memorialize that meeting by using Form 510 and ensure that the employee returns a signed copy of the memo to you.

If that meeting and notice do not do the job, hold a second meeting with the employee and go through the problem and the solutions you are looking for once again. Use Form 511 to memorialize this meeting (remember to get a signed copy of the notice).

If the second meeting does not produce the desired results, then you have two options. If the employee is making an effort to comply with your wishes and you are not yet prepared to fire that person, you may wish to hold a third meeting and use a variation of Form 511 to give the employee a last chance. If you've concluded that the employee will not work out the problem, then you should use Form 512 to notify the employee that he or she is being fired.

EMPLOYMENT REFERENCE REQUEST

Date:

Dear   :

                has applied to us seeking a position as
. Your firm has been listed by the applicant as a prior
employer.

By means of this letter, we are requesting a reference on the applicant
including but not limited to the dates the applicant was employed by you, the date
the individual left your employment, a rating of his or her performance and the
reason the applicant left your employ.

A consent form executed by the applicant is enclosed.

Your prompt consideration is greatly appreciated.

                Sincerely,

_____

APPLICANT CHECKLIST

1. Name:
2. Address:
3. Job Station:
4. References:
   Previous Employers: Date Requested: Date Received:

5. Interview Process:
   Interviewer: Recommendation:

6. Credentials:
   Education: Licenses: Date Validated:

7. Starting Salary:
8. Benefits Package:
9. Commencement Date:

MEDICAL CONSENT

I, the undersigned individual, asserting that I am over the age of majority, in consideration for employment with   , do, for the limited purpose of consideration of employment, authorize the following medical examination:

     I recognize that the medical examination is for the benefit of my prospective employer and will be included as a part of its determination whether to extend employment to me.

     I release   and the medical professional who will conduct such tests from all liability for diagnosis and treatment. I authorize this consent without limitation or uncertainty.

Date: _____

_____

LETTER OF EMPLOYMENT

Date:

Dear   :

It is with pleasure that we inform you of your appointment as
                    with our firm. Your immediate supervisor will be
                                        . The
starting date of your employment is   , 19   .

Your annual compensation will be   dollars ($), which
will be paid on a   basis.

You will be entitled, on a yearly basis, to   (   ) days of vacation time
and   (   ) days of paid sick leave.

Furthermore, you will be a participant in the employee benefit plans to which
you are eligible. They will be explained in greater detail when you are eligible to
participate.

THIS CONTRACT IS FOR EMPLOYMENT AT WILL. IT MAY BE
TERMINATED EITHER BY YOU OR BY US FOR ANY REASON AT ANY
TIME.

Kindly acknowledge your acceptance of this offer by signing your name after
the words "Agreed to and accepted" and return the enclosed copy of this letter to
us at the address shown above.

Sincerely,

_____

Agreed to and accepted: _____

SALES EMPLOYMENT AGREEMENT

EMPLOYMENT AGREEMENT, effective this   day of   , 19   ,
by and between   (hereinafter referred to as the
"Company"), a corporation organized and existing under the laws of the state of
                , with its principal place of business located at
           , and   , (hereinafter referred to as the
"Employee"), an individual, with his or her principal residence located at

WITNESSETH:

WHEREAS, the Company is in the business of   ; and

WHEREAS, the operation by the Company of its business requires disclosure
of confidential information to its employees; and

WHEREAS, such confidential information provided to the Employee by the
Company if improperly used by the Employee for his or her own purpose rather
than on behalf of the Company can result in irreparable harm to the Company,
which harm, because of the nature of the industry, is not susceptible to precise
proof; and

WHEREAS, the training of the Employee by the Company, the skills obtained
by the Employee and the disclosure to the Employee of such aforesaid confidential
information makes such Employee valuable to competitors of the Company; and

WHEREAS, the Employee is desirous of entering into the employment of the
Company and is aware of the foregoing consideration and understands the reasons
for the terms and conditions of his or her employment as set forth below.

NOW, THEREFORE, in consideration of the premises and mutual covenants
and promises set forth herein, and intending to be legally bound hereby, the parties
agree as follows:

ARTICLE I: PURPOSES. The Company hereby employs the Employee and
the Employee accepts employment from the Company as a salesperson and/or
such other duties as the Company may, from time to time, determine.

The Company hereby engages the Employee for the primary purpose of
soliciting   sales in the territory or territories to be determined
by the Company at the Company's sole discretion.

ARTICLE II: DUTIES. The Employee accepts such employment as a salesperson and agrees to devote his or her full-time and best efforts to soliciting sales in the territory or territories to be determined by the Company.

The Employee shall solicit   sales for the exclusive benefit of the Company and perform such other duties as may be assigned to him or her by the Company. The Employee agrees that during the term of this agreement, he or she will have no other employment except as may be specifically authorized in writing by the Company. The Employee shall not serve as an adviser, agent, consultant, independent contractor or in any other capacity with respect to any trade or business, proprietorship, partnership, corporation or other entity, person or firm that directly sells or services   or any type of product or service that competes, conflicts or interferes with the performance of his or her duties, unless he or she has first received written consent of the Company, which consent shall be revocable at the will of the Company.

The Employee shall present the Company's line of to prospective clients and will offer such at prices furnished by the Company, on the terms and conditions established by the Company and in the territories established by the Company.

The Employee shall not at any time enter into any contract with any person, firm or corporation that shall purport to bind the Company in any manner whatsoever without written authority from the Company and any such contract entered into by such Employee shall not be binding upon the Company. The Company specifically reserves the right to reject any contract or to cancel any contract or part thereof, even after acceptance, for credit reasons or for any other reason whatsoever that the Company may deem appropriate.

ARTICLE III: TERMS. The Company hereby employs the Employee and the Employee hereby accepts employment for a term of   (   ) year(s) from the date hereof unless terminated by either party by written notice sent by certified mail at least   (   ) days in advance of such termination. Such notice of termination shall not prejudice either party as to any remedies under the provisions of this agreement. If the agreement is not terminated by either party during the initial term hereof, the Employee's employment shall continue thereafter under the terms and conditions hereof for a period of one year, and so on from year to year, until either party terminates this agreement.

ARTICLE IV: COMPENSATION. As compensation for all of the services to be rendered by the Employee pursuant to the terms and conditions set forth herein and such other duties as the Company may from time to time determine, the Employee shall receive a commission in an amount to be determined pursuant to the Schedule(s) of Commissions to be published by the Company, from time to time.

In the event that a commission is paid to the Employee pursuant to the terms of this ARTICLE IV, and the Company, for whatever reason whatsoever, is thereafter obligated to return the payments upon which the commission is determined, the Employee shall, upon thirty (30) days' written notice, repay to the Company such compensation as he or she has received based on the amounts so returned or returnable. Compensation payable pursuant to this ARTICLE IV shall be paid not less frequently than monthly and may be offset by any amounts owed to the Company.

In the event the Company shall determine, in its sole discretion, that compensation based on the Schedule of Commissions shall change, the Company shall provide written notice to the Employee at least thirty (30) days prior to the said change. The Company agrees that it shall not change the commission schedule unless the said changes are made for all sales employees of the Company.

Any amounts paid and any benefits provided to the Employee pursuant to this agreement that are deemed to be compensation under the Internal Revenue Code shall be subject to the applicable income tax withholding for federal, state and local income taxes. In addition, the Company shall deduct from the compensation paid to the Employee such other deductions as authorized by the Employee or by a court of competent jurisdiction.

ARTICLE V: OTHER BENEFITS AND EXPENSES. The Employee shall be entitled during the term of this agreement to participate in all health insurance and benefit plans, group insurance or other plan or plans providing benefits generally applicable to the employees of the Company who are currently in existence or those who hereafter may be adopted by the Company.

Once the Employee shall be deemed a "successful salesperson," said determination to be at the sole discretion of the Company as applied to all salespeople, the Employee may draw for expenses up to   dollars ($) per month, the said draw amount being subject to change as long as the said change applies to all "successful salespeople" at the sole discretion of the

Company. The Employee shall submit evidence of the said expenses on no less than a monthly basis with the difference between the monthly draw and the actual verified expenses being returned to the Company within thirty (30) days of notice.

ARTICLE VI: PRICES AND SERVICE. The Employee shall sell the Company's   at the price and under the terms and conditions established by the Company. Said prices, terms and conditions may, from time to time, be changed and/or modified by the Company at its sole discretion. The Employee shall not at any time enter into any contract with any person, firm or corporation that shall purport to bind the Company in any manner whatsoever without written authority from the Company and any such contract entered into by such Employee shall not be binding upon the Company. The Company specifically reserves the right to reject any application or contract or to cancel any application or contract or part thereof even after acceptance, for credit reasons or for any other reason whatsoever that the Company deems appropriate.

ARTICLE VII: TERMINATION. In the event of the death of the Employee, the Company shall pay to the representative of the Employee's estate all funds due to the Employee to the date of death. In the event that the Employee becomes disabled because of physical or mental disability as to be unable to perform the services required by this agreement and such disability continues for   (   ) days, the Company may, at or after the expiration of such   (   )-day period and provided that the Employee's incapacity is then continuing, terminate the Employee's employment under this agreement. It is expressly understood that the inability of the Employee to render services to the Company by reason of illness, disability or incapacity or any cause beyond his or her control shall not constitute a failure by the Employee to perform his or her obligations hereunder and shall not be considered a breach or default under this agreement.

In the event that the Employee violates any of the provisions of this agreement or performs any act or does anything by which the Company shall incur liability, then, at the option of the Company, this contract shall at once cease and the Company shall be under no obligation to the Employee, except to pay the Employee for such services as may have been performed up to the date of termination of this agreement as herein provided.

In the event that the Employee violates any of the provisions of this agreement or fails to perform the services required of the Employee by this agreement, then at the option of the Company, this agreement shall at once cease and become null and void and the Company shall be under no obligation to said Employee except to pay the Employee such compensation as he or she may be entitled to receive up to the time of such termination.

In the event that the Employee becomes insolvent and unable to pay his or her debts in full or files a petition in bankruptcy or is adjudicated a bankrupt, this agreement shall at once cease and become null and void and the Company shall be under no obligation to the Employee except to pay the Employee such compensation as he or she may be entitled to receive up to the time of such termination.

In the event that the Employee should be arrested or be the subject to an indictment or charged with any crime or unlawful act involving an allegation or charge of a breach of moral turpitude or the sale or use of a prohibited drug or controlled substance, this contract shall at once cease and become null and void and the Company shall be under no obligation to the Employee except to pay the Employee such compensation as he or she may be entitled to receive up to the time of such termination.

In the event that the Employee should be found to have taken, used or converted any property belonging to the Company, the Employee shall be immediately discharged and this contract shall at once cease and become null and void and the Company shall be under no obligation to the Employee except to pay the Employee such compensation as he or she may be entitled to receive up to the time of such termination.

Any payments due the Employee pursuant to termination shall be paid to the Employee as soon as the Company can determine the true and correct amount for all payments due the Employee, except that in the event that said termination is due to the misconduct of the Employee pertaining to any of the terms hereunder, the Company shall have the right to withhold all money due the Employee and shall apply said funds as an offset against any money due the Company from the Employee as a result of the Employee misconduct. In any event, the Employee shall be entitled to an accounting, in writing, of the funds so withheld.

ARTICLE VIII: CONFIDENTIAL INFORMATION. "Confidential Information" shall be defined for the purpose of this agreement as information (1) disclosed to the Employee or known or gathered by the Employee as a consequence of or through his or her employment by the Company and (2) not generally known to the industry in which the Company is or may become engaged about the Company's products, administrative services or methods of doing business, including, but not limited to, information relating to trade secrets, marketing techniques and programs, dates, figures, projections, costs, methods of operation, identity of plans or administrative services, estimates, customer lists, customer history, personnel history, financial statements, accounting procedures and selling techniques.

That the Employee will not during his or her employment or after termination thereof, irrespective of the time, manner or cause of the termination of said employment, directly or indirectly disclose to any person, firm or corporation any of the above Confidential Information that he or she shall have acquired during his or her term of employment.

The Employee agrees that he or she will not, during his or her employment by the Company or at any time thereafter, interfere with or disrupt, or attempt to interfere with or disrupt, any business relationship, contractual or otherwise, between the Company and any other party, including clients or prospective clients, suppliers, agents or the employees of the Company.

The Employee acknowledges that all documents, words, files, customer lists, information and data in his or her possession or custody, whether gathered by the Employee or any other person, and whether or not reduced to writing, an electronic or magnetic medium, relating to the business activities of the Company are and shall remain the sole and exclusive property of the Company and/or the Company's customers.

That upon the termination of said employment, irrespective of the time, manner or cause of said termination, the Employee will surrender to the Company all information written or otherwise in connection with the Company's customers or business as well as other property of the Company.

ARTICLE IX: NONCOMPETITION PROVISION. In further consideration of employment, the Employee shall not engage in a business in any manner similar to or in competition with the Company's or the Company's affiliated businesses during the term of his or her employment. Furthermore, the Employee shall not engage in a business in any manner similar to or in competition with the Company's business for a period of   (   ) years from the date of termination of his or her employment with the Company in the geographic area within a

      (   )-mile radius of any present or future office opened by the Company during the term of employment and the geographic area within a ( )-mile radius of the Employee's home address.

The Employee shall not request any customers of any business then being conducted or contemplated by the Company or its affiliates to curtail or cancel their business with the Company or its affiliates.

The Employee shall not disclose to any person, firm or corporation any trade, technical or technologic secrets, any details of organizations or business affairs, any names of past or present customers of the Company or its affiliates or any other information relating to the business or businesses or their affiliates.

The Employee shall not solicit, canvass or accept any business or transaction for any other person, firm or corporation or business similar to any business of the Company or its affiliates.

The Employee shall not induce, or attempt to influence, any employee of the business or its affiliates to terminate employment with the business or its affiliates or to enter into any employment or other business relationship with any other person (including the Employee), firm or corporation.

The Employee shall not act or conduct himself or herself in any manner that he or she shall have reason to believe is inimical or contrary to the best interests of the Company or its affiliates.

The Employee shall not perform any act in violation hereof through any other person or entity or through any plan, scheme or design calculated to circumvent the requirements hereof.

The Employee acknowledges and agrees that the above restriction is reasonable as to duration and geography, that it is fully enforceable, and waives any objection thereto and covenants to institute no suit or proceeding or otherwise advance any position or contention to the contrary.

The Employee recognizes that immediate and irreparable damage will result to the Company if the Employee breaches any of the terms and conditions of this article and, accordingly, the Employee hereby consents to the entry of temporary, preliminary and permanent injunctive relief by any court of competent jurisdiction against him or her to restrain any such breach, in addition to any other remedies or claims for money damages that the Company may seek; and the Employee agrees to render an equitable accounting of all earnings, profits and other benefits arising from such violations; and to pay all costs and counsel fees incurred by the Company in enforcing this agreement, which rights shall be cumulative. The

Employee represents and warrants to the Company that his or her experience and capabilities are such that he or she can obtain employment in business without breaching the terms and conditions of this article and that his or her obligations under the provisions of this article (and the enforcement thereof by injunction or otherwise) will not prevent him or her from earning a livelihood.

This covenant on the part of the Employee shall be construed as an agreement independent of any other provisions of this agreement, and the existence of any claim or cause of action of the Employee against the Company, whether predicated on this agreement or otherwise, shall not constitute a defense to the enforcement by the Company of this covenant.

In the event that the Employee is in breach of any of the provisions of this Article IX, the period of proscription from doing the act or acts that constitute a breach of this Article IX shall be extended for a period of two (2) years from the date that the Employee ceased, whether voluntarily or by court order, to engage in or do said actions.

The Employee recognizes and agrees that the Company does not have a remedy at law adequate to protect the Company's rights and interests as set forth in this article, and the Employee therefore agrees that the Company shall have the right to an injunction enjoining the Employee from violating the provisions of this article. Nothing herein contained shall be construed as prohibiting the Company from pursuing any other remedies available to the Company for such breach or threatened breach, including the recovery of damages from the Employee.

If any action at law or equity is necessary to enforce or interpret the terms of this agreement, the Employee agrees to pay the Company reasonable attorney's fees, costs and necessary disbursements, in addition to any other relief and/or damages to which the Company may be entitled.

In the event that a court of competent jurisdiction determines that this restrictive covenant and covenant not to compete is unenforceable in whole or in part for any reason, including, without limitation, the duration, scope and remedies set forth above, then same shall not be void, but rather shall be enforced to the extent that same is deemed to be enforceable by said court, as if originally executed in that form by the parties hereto.

ARTICLE X: MISCELLANEOUS. Service of all notice under this agreement shall be sufficient if made by registered mail to the specific party involved herein at his or her respective address hereinafter set forth or as such party may provide from time to time in writing:

For the Company:

For the Employee:

This agreement constitutes the entire agreement between the parties hereto and supersedes all prior negotiations, understandings and agreements, whether oral or written, of any nature whatsoever with respect to the term of employment that is the subject matter hereof, and there are no representations, warranties, understandings or agreements other than those expressly set forth herein between the Company and the Employee. This agreement cannot be changed, modified or terminated except in writing and signed by the parties hereto.

The validity, interpretation, construction and enforcement of this agreement shall be governed by the laws of the state of   .

The Company shall have the right, but not the obligation, to assign this agreement and the Company's rights hereunder in whole, but not in part, to any corporation or other entity with or into which the Company may hereafter merge or consolidate or to which the Company may transfer all or substantially all of its assets provided such corporation or other entity assumes all of the Company's obligations hereunder.

The Employee understands and acknowledges that his or her employment contract is a contract for personal services of the Employee and cannot be assigned.

This contract is for the personal services of the Employee and shall cease and desist and be considered null and void upon the termination of the contract under any of the provisions hereto.

The invalidity or unenforceability of any particular provision of this agreement shall not affect the other provisions hereto and the agreement shall be construed in all respects as though such invalid or unenforceable provision were omitted.

Any legal action undertaken by the Employee pursuant to any of the terms or conditions or the interpretation thereof shall be commenced within six (6) months of said termination. The Employee agrees hereby that after a term of six (6) months has expired, no legal action against the Company may be brought in any court regarding any term or condition of this agreement.

IN WITNESS WHEREOF, the parties hereto acknowledge, understand and agree to this Employment Agreement. The parties understand and intend to be bound by all of the clauses contained in this document and further certify that they have received signed copies of this agreement.

Company By:

_____

President

_____

Employee

EXPENSE REIMBURSEMENT CONTRACT

Date:

The undersigned officer or shareholder/employee agrees to reimburse

_____ (the Company) for expenses that are determined by the Internal Revenue Service not to constitute a deductible business expense pursuant to the Internal Revenue Code of 1986, as amended. The amount to be repaid shall be an amount equal to that which is disallowed by the Internal Revenue Service, upon a final determination of such disallowance.

_____

EXPENSE ACCOUNT REPORT

Employee:

Department:

Expenses authorized by:

Period covered:

Purpose of meal or trip:

Companies or individuals visited:

Specific Expenses

Hotels/Motels:	$
Meals:	$
Tips:	$
Auto Expense:	
Mileage at ¢ per mile	$
Tolls	$
Parking	$
Telephone:	$
Miscellaneous:	$
Entertainment:*	$
Total Expenses:	$

*List persons entertained, nature of entertainment and results of the meeting:

_____

Employee

Reviewed and approved:

_____

Date approved: _____

EMPLOYEE'S CONSENT TO DISCLOSE INFORMATION

Date:

I, _____, have been informed that my current employer has
been requested to provide information about my employment from

_____ .

I hereby authorize my employer to release the information without limitation.

_____

NONCOMPETITION CONTRACT

IN CONSIDERATION OF EMPLOYMENT AND OTHER VALUABLE CONSIDERATION that is acknowledged, the undersigned, (hereinafter "Employee") shall not engage in a business in any manner similar to or in competition with   (hereinafter the "Company") or the Company's affiliated businesses during the term of his or her employment. Furthermore, the Employee shall not engage in a business in any manner similar to or in competition with the Company's business for a period of   (   ) years from the date of termination of his or her employment with the Company in the geographic area within a   (   )-mile radius of any present or future office opened by the Company during the term of employment and the geographic area within a   (   )-mile radius of the Employee's home address.

For the purpose of this agreement, the Employee shall be regarded as engaging in a "business in any manner similar to or in competition with the Company's business" if, directly or as an independent contractor or employee of any business, the Employee is engaged in the business of   or such other business or businesses as the Company is engaged in either individually or as part of some other business entity or affiliate during the term of the Employee's employment by the Company.

The Employee shall not request any customers of any business then being conducted or contemplated by the Company or its affiliates to curtail or cancel their business with the business or its affiliates.

The Employee shall not disclose to any person, firm or corporation any trade, technical or technologic secrets, any details of organizations or business affairs, any names of past or present customers of the Company or its affiliates or any other information relating to the business or businesses or their affiliates.

The Employee shall not solicit, canvass or accept any business or transaction for any other person, firm or corporation or business similar to any business of the Company or its affiliates.

The Employee shall not induce, or attempt to influence, any employee of the Company or its affiliates to terminate employment with the Company or its affiliates or to enter into any employment or other business relationship with any other person (including the Employee), firm or corporation.

The Employee shall not act or conduct himself or herself in any manner that he or she shall have reason to believe is inimical or contrary to the best interests of the Company or its affiliates.

The Employee shall not perform any act in violation hereof through any other person or entity, or through any plan, scheme or design calculated to circumvent the requirements hereof.

The Employee acknowledges and agrees that the above restriction is reasonable as to duration and geography, that it is fully enforceable, and waives any objection thereto and covenants to institute no suit or proceeding or otherwise advance any position or contention to the contrary.

The Employee recognizes that immediate and irreparable damage will result to the Company if the Employee breaches any of the terms and conditions of this agreement and, accordingly, the Employee hereby consents to the entry of temporary, preliminary and permanent injunctive relief by any court of competent jurisdiction against him or her to restrain any such breach, in addition to any other remedies or claims for money damages that the Company may seek; and the Employee agrees to render an equitable accounting of all earnings, profits and other benefits arising from such violations; and to pay all costs and counsel fees incurred by the Company in enforcing this agreement, which rights shall be cumulative.

The Employee represents and warrants to the Company that his or her experience and capabilities are such that he or she can obtain employment in business without breaching the terms and conditions of this agreement and that his or her obligations under the provisions of this agreement (and the enforcement thereof by injunction or otherwise) will not prevent him or her from earning a livelihood.

The existence of any claim or cause of action of the Employee against the Company, whether predicated on this agreement or otherwise, shall not constitute a defense to the enforcement by the Company of this covenant.

In the event that the Employee is in breach of any of the provisions of this agreement as set forth above, the period of proscription from doing the act or acts that constitute a breach of this agreement shall be extended for a period of (   ) years from the date that the Employee ceased, whether voluntarily or by court order, to engage in or do said actions.

The Employee recognizes and agrees that the Company does not have a remedy at law adequate to protect the Company's rights and interests as set forth in this agreement, and the Employee therefore agrees that the Company shall have the right to an injunction enjoining the Employee from violating the provisions of this agreement. Nothing herein contained shall be construed as prohibiting the Company from pursuing any other remedies available to the Company for such breach or threatened breach.

If any action at law or equity is necessary to enforce or interpret the terms of this agreement, the Employee agrees to pay the Company reasonable attorney's fees, costs and necessary disbursements, in addition to any other relief and/or damages to which the Company may be entitled.

In the event that a court of competent jurisdiction determines that this covenant not to compete is unenforceable in whole or in part for any reason, including, without limitation, the duration, scope and remedies set forth above, then same shall not be void, but rather shall be enforced to the extent that same is deemed to be enforceable by said court, as if originally executed in that form by the parties hereto.

Service of all notice under this agreement shall be sufficient if made by registered mail to the specific party involved herein at his or her respective address hereinafter set forth or as such party may provide from time to time in writing:

For the Company:

For the Employee:

This agreement constitutes the entire agreement between the parties hereto and supersedes all prior negotiations, understandings and agreements, whether oral or written, of any nature whatsoever with respect to the term of employment that is the subject matter hereof, and there are no representations, warranties, understandings or agreements other than those expressly set forth herein between the Company and the Employee.

This agreement is not to be changed, modified or terminated except in writing and signed by the parties hereto.

The validity, interpretation, construction and enforcement of this agreement shall be governed by the laws of the state of

The invalidity or unenforceability of any particular provision of this agreement shall not affect the other provisions hereto and the agreement shall be construed in all respects as though such invalid or unenforceable provision were omitted.

IN WITNESS WHEREOF, the parties hereto acknowledge, understand and agree to this agreement. The parties understand and intend to be bound by all of the clauses contained in this document and further certify that they have received signed copies of this agreement on this date.

Employee:

_____

For the Company:

_____

(Notary Public)

ACKNOWLEDGMENT

This acknowledgment shall be attached to and considered part of the employment agreement executed this date by and between Company and the Employee,

The Employee recognizes, understands and specifically agrees to the (   )-year restrictive covenant contained in the foregoing agreement. The Employee further acknowledges that said   (   )-year restrictive covenant and the geographic limitations set forth therein is reasonable.

I UNDERSTAND AND AGREE THAT I WILL NOT COMPETE IN ANY MANNER AGAINST THE COMPANY, DIRECTLY OR INDIRECTLY FOR A PERIOD OF   (   ) YEARS FROM THE TIME I LEAVE, VOLUNTARILY OR BY TERMINATION, THE EMPLOYMENT OF THE COMPANY.

I understand that my employment with the Company is absolutely conditioned upon execution of this Acknowledgment and agreement. I have fully read, understand and agree to be bound by the attached agreement and this Acknowledgment. I,   , hereby further acknowledge and confirm that I have read and understand the foregoing agreement. I understand that I have the right and the time to have this agreement reviewed by legal counsel of my choice but decline to do so.

IN WITNESS WHEREOF, and intending to be legally bound hereby, the Employee has set his or her hand and seal on this   day of   , 19   , and hereby acknowledges, understands and agrees to the above.

Employee: _____

(Notary Public) _____

NOTICE OF WORK-PERFORMANCE DEFICIENCIES

Date:

To:

This letter confirms our recent meeting of   , 19   , when we discussed your poor job performance. You were cautioned that your performance was not acceptable in the following respects:

Based on the above factors, you have been given an unsatisfactory performance rating. For you to enjoy a good status standing, you must improve your performance and, as we discussed, adopt the following action plan to improve your performance:

We trust that this notice is accepted as constructive and that we can look forward to improved performance on your part.

As you will note, a copy of this notice has been attached. Please sign that copy where indicated and return it to me promptly.

Sincerely,

_____

Receipt acknowledged: _____

FINAL DISMISSAL NOTICE

Date:

To:

You have been counseled and warned of deficiencies in your job performance (see notification dated   , 19   , a copy of which is attached).

Regretfully, the deficiencies do not seem to have been corrected. Immediate action, in conformity with the earlier notification mentioned above, must be taken by you to correct your performance deficiencies. I cannot stress too strongly that such action must be undertaken without delay. Failure to comply will result in your dismissal without additional notice.

I have attached a copy of this notice; please sign where indicated and return the copy to me promptly.

_____

Receipt acknowledged: _____

Employee

DISMISSAL NOTIFICATION

Date:

To:

This memorandum confirms the conversation we had earlier on   ,
19   , during which you were advised that your services for the company will not
be required after   , 19   , and that your employment with the
company will terminate on that date.

    This action was taken for the following reason(s):

    Severance pay and accrued benefits shall continue pursuant to the company's
specific benefit program and in conformity with the law. Please make an
appointment with   , so that we may discuss the
termination procedure and your right to benefits.

    I have attached a copy of this notice; please sign the copy where indicated and
promptly return the copy to me.

    We wish you well in your future endeavors.

Sincerely,

               _____

Receipt acknowledged: _____

             Employee

CHAPTER 6

Buying and Selling Goods

Introduction

Most daily business transactions are governed by Article 2 of the UCC. This article is so extensive that it may even add terms to a contract where the contract is silent on those terms. This chapter provides forms that will protect your rights under the UCC and preserve any remedies that you may have if the other party breaches a contract.

The Initial Order

All of the forms in this chapter should be prepared on your business stationery. Form 601 asks a supplier for a firm price on goods that you wish to purchase. This form will obligate a supplier, in the event you purchase, to the prices the supplier has submitted. Form 602 can be used by a supplier to inform a customer that goods ordered by the customer will be shipped cash on delivery (COD). If the supplier does not supply this information, the buyer may have the right to expect that he or she will be billed after delivery.

Form 603 should be used by the buyer to confirm a telephone order; by using it, you will avoid any misunderstanding regarding quality, quantity, price, credit and delivery terms. Form 604 is the seller's version of Form 603 and serves the same purpose as that form. Form 605 should be used in place of Form 604 if the buyer's entire order will be filled with more than one shipment.

Form 606 is designed for sellers who have received orders without shipping instructions. If a buyer does not respond to the seller's request for shipping instructions, the seller is not obliged to ship the order. Form 607 notifies the purchaser that the goods are being held and supplies a checklist of reasons for the seller's decision not to ship.

Forms 608 and 609 should be used for approval or consignment sales. Each form sets out the terms of the transaction. Should the purchaser return goods accepted on approval (Form 608), he or she should use Form 610 to return the goods.

Delivery and Cancellation

In Form 611, the buyer acknowledges that the goods he or she purchased were received and are acceptable. Before issuing this receipt you must ensure that you have had adequate time to carefully inspect the goods. If the goods later turn out to be faulty in some respect, the receipt you issued may weaken any claim you may have against the supplier.

Form 612 should be used when the parties agree to amend the terms of the purchase contract. The buyer or seller who initiates this form should mail two signed copies of the form so that the other party can return a signed copy. Suppliers can use Form 613 to notify their customers of delivery dates. There is no legal requirement calling for a shipping notice; however, it does help to promote good relationships.

Form 614 can be used by a buyer to cancel items that the supplier has put on back order. This right is provided to buyers by the UCC, but you must exercise it promptly.

Forms 615 and 616 deal with the delivery of goods. Failure to make delivery pursuant to the purchase contract is generally considered a breach of the contract. Form 615 should be used when the buyer has made payment. Form 616 should be used by the buyer to ask the seller to supply delivery dates, and it retains the buyer's right to cancel the order if the seller does not supply a delivery date.

Form 617 adopts a checklist format that buyers can use to reject goods that were delivered. The UCC provides the purchaser with remedies for nonconforming items. The primary remedy is rejection, which you may use to reject all or a part of the shipment.

Forms 618 through 620 deal with damaged goods. The purchaser has the option under the UCC to reject or retain the goods. Form 618 assumes the buyer will accept the damaged goods, but wants an allowance on the price. If the seller does not agree to a reduced price, the buyer still retains the right to reject the goods.

A seller who has received notice that the buyer will not or has not accepted delivery can use Form 619 to respond to the buyer and preserve the seller's rights against the buyer for a breach of contract.

Form 620 is a notice of resale. One remedy the UCC provides to suppliers is to permit the seller to sell items in question and then to look to the buyer for any deficiency between the sale and the contract price.

Form 621 can be used by a seller to advise a shipping company to stop the shipment of goods. Unless a "Negotiable Bill of Lading" has been given to the purchaser, the seller has an absolute right to stop a shipment.

Return and Disputes

If your customer becomes insolvent within ten days of the date that he or she receives a shipment from you, the UCC gives you the right to demand a return of the goods included in the shipment. Form 622 should be used by suppliers to demand that insolvent customers return delivered goods.

Form 623 should be used by purchasers to notify their suppliers of a disagreement regarding their outstanding account balance. Purchasers should be careful to monitor their bills because a failure to challenge the amounts set out in your bills may act as an admission of the amounts claimed by the supplier. Form 624 should be used by a purchaser whenever a dispute about the account balance exists. Even if the check you send states that it is in payment of specific invoices, you still should use this form to direct your creditor to apply the payment to specified, undisputed accounts.

BID REQUEST

Date:

To:

Kindly provide us with your bid for the following items:

Item	Quantity	Unit Price	Total Price
_____	_____	$ _____	$ _____
_____	_____	$ _____	$ _____
_____	_____	$ _____	$ _____
_____	_____	$ _____	$ _____
_____	_____	$ _____	$ _____
_____	_____	$ _____	$ _____

Please quote your bid delivery to us free on board (FOB) at the following location:

If your bid prices will not remain firm for at least thirty (30) days, please advise us of when the bid price no longer will be effective.

Sincerely,

_____

NOTICE THAT SALE WILL BE ON COD TERMS

Date:

To:

We welcome your patronage and acknowledge receipt of your order for goods. With respect to payment terms, please be advised that we will ship your order cash on delivery (COD) ten (10) days from the date of this letter, unless you cancel the order or make other financing arrangements within the next ten (10) days.

Thank you for your order; we hope we can continue to be of service to you.

Sincerely,

_____

ORDER CONFIRMATION

Date:

To:

Dear   :

This will confirm our order of   ,19   , which we placed
with you by telephone. A purchase order authorizing the order on the terms that
we discussed is attached to this letter.

If any of the terms set out in the purchase order no longer are acceptable to
you, please advise us within ten (10) days of the date of this letter; otherwise, we
shall deem the order accepted in due form and we will anticipate prompt delivery.

Sincerely,

_____

ACCEPTANCE OF AN ORDER

Date:

To:

Dear   :

Receipt of your purchase order number   is hereby acknowledged.

    This will confirm that we have accepted your order with the following exceptions:

    Unless we receive written notice from you within   (   ) days, we shall assume that you have accepted our exceptions and we will fulfill the order according to the above exceptions.

    Your business is greatly appreciated. Thank you.

                Sincerely,

_____

ACCEPTANCE OF AN ORDER
(SHIPMENT IN MORE THAN ONE LOT)

Date:

To:

Dear   :

Receipt of your purchase order dated   , 19   , is hereby
noticed. The items that you ordered will be shipped in the following different lots:

Payment will be due for each lot as it is delivered.

Sincerely,

_____

REQUEST FOR SHIPPING INSTRUCTIONS

Date:

To:-

Dear   :

Your order is important to us. Although we are prepared to fulfill it promptly, you have not provided delivery instructions.

Kindly provide such directions by return mail, or we shall have to hold your order.

Sincerely,

_____

NOTIFICATION OF NONSHIPMENT

Date:

To:

Dear   :

We are holding shipment of your order dated   , 19   , for
the following reason(s):

    [ ] Nonpayment.

    [ ] No shipping directions provided.

    [ ] Your contract has been canceled.

    [ ] The following items are on back order:

    [ ] Other:

Sincerely,

_____

SALE SUBJECT TO APPROVAL

Date:

To:

Dear   :

Thank you for your order of   . Your request for delivery of
goods on an approval basis is hereby accepted. You have the right to return the
items shipped under the attached invoice within   (   ) days of delivery. Any
items not so returned will be considered accepted.

    We look forward to doing additional business with you in the future.

Sincerely,

_____

CONSIGNMENT SALE

Date:

To:

Dear   :

In accordance with your invoice (copy attached), we are shipping the goods you ordered on a consignment basis. Any goods not sold by you may be returned to us for credit. If any such goods are returned, you shall be responsible for the cost of shipping those goods to us.

This consignment agreement also includes the following terms:

1. We retain the right to the immediate return of any unsold goods.
2. You have agreed to sign any financing agreements that are needed to protect our ownership rights.
3. All items that you sell under this consignment are subject to the payment terms set out in the attached invoice.

Please indicate that you have accepted the terms of this consignment agreement by signing below under the words "Agreed to and accepted" and returning a signed copy to me by return mail.

Sincerely,

_____

Agreed to and accepted:

_____

NOTICE: RETURN OF APPROVAL-SALE PRODUCTS

Date:

To:

Dear   :

We are returning to you the following goods that you delivered to us on approval
on   , 19   .

    The returned items are:

    We thank you for the opportunity to review your goods.

                Sincerely,

            _____

RECEIPT FOR DELIVERY OF GOODS

Date:

To:

Dear   :

We hereby acknowledge that the items listed on the attached form have been received by us, inspected by us and are accepted by us as in good form without defect.

Sincerely,

_____

MODIFICATION OF A CONTRACT

Date:

To:

Dear   :

This letter will serve as the written modification of our contract dated
                    , 19   . The contract is revised as follows:

If the above comports with your understanding of our agreement to modify our contract, please sign below under the words "Agreed to and accepted" and return a signed copy of this letter to us at the address shown above.

Sincerely,

_____

Agreed to and accepted:

_____

SHIPPING NOTICE

Date:

To:

Dear   :

We shipped the items you ordered (see your purchase order numbered   ) on

                    , 19   . You can expect your order to arrive at your offices

on   , 19   .

    Your business is greatly appreciated.

                            Sincerely,

                            _____

NOTICE OF CANCELLATION: BACK-ORDERED ITEMS

Date:

To:

Dear   :

You have notified us that certain items on our purchase order, number   , dated   , 19   , are not in your stock and have been back ordered.

Because timely receipt of the items is a necessity for us, please cancel the back-ordered items from our order and ship the remainder of the order immediately. Please ensure that the invoice you send to us reflects the fact that we have canceled the order for the items you have on back order.

Sincerely,

_____

DEMAND FOR DELIVERY AFTER PAYMENT

Date:

To:

Dear   :

We acted in good faith and have paid   dollars ($), the
full purchase price of the items that we ordered from your firm on
        , 19   . Payment was made on   , 19   .

To date, however, we have not received delivery.

We hereby demand immediate delivery.

Sincerely,

_____

DEMAND FOR SHIPPING DATES

Date:

To:

Dear   :

Pursuant to our contract dated   , 19   , we require you to
provide us with the arrangements that you have made to ship the goods that we
ordered to us and that you also provide adequate security that you will conform to
those arrangements.

    Should you be unable to provide such information and security, you will be in
violation of the above-described contract and we may choose to terminate it
pursuant to its terms.

        Sincerely,

_____

NOTICE: REJECTION OF SHIPMENT

Date:

To:

Dear   :

We are in receipt of the items that you shipped to us on   ,

19   . The items are rejected for the following reasons:

[ ]   The items were delivered in damaged condition (see explanation attached).

[ ]   The items delivered are defective (see attached explanation).

[ ]   The shipment was not timely delivered.

[ ]   The items were not in compliance with the purchase order (see attached explanation).

[ ]   The prices on your invoice are not in compliance with the purchase order accepted by your firm.

[ ]   The entire order was not shipped; no back orders are acceptable.

[ ]   Other:

This rejection does not act to limit or waiver any other legal right that we may have.

Because this order was prepaid, we demand that you issue a credit for the full amount paid to your company.

Sincerely,

_____

NOTICE: ACCEPTANCE OF DAMAGED GOODS

Date:

To:

Dear   :

We are in receipt of certain items pursuant to our purchase order dated
_____, 19____. The following items arrived damaged or defective
in the following respects:

    Pursuant to our conversation, we have agreed to accept said items subject to
an adjustment of _____ dollars ($_____) in the purchase price.
Kindly issue a new invoice showing the adjustment and correct our account
accordingly.

Sincerely,

_____

SUPPLIER'S RESPONSE TO NONACCEPTANCE

Date:

To:

Dear   :

We acknowledge that you have refused to accept delivery of the items that you ordered. Accordingly, we shall restock the items in our inventory. However, we reserve the right to proceed against you for your breach of contract for all foreseeable and resulting damages.

Sincerely,

_____

NOTICE OF RESALE BY SELLER

Date:

To:

Dear   :

As you have breached the contract dated   , 19   , which you made with us, this letter is written to inform you that the items that you ordered will be sold on   , 19   .

The items will be sold to the highest bidder. If the purchase price at the sale is less than the price set out in the above-described contract, you will be required to satisfy any shortfall.

Sincerely,

_____

STOP SHIPMENT ORDER

Date:

To:

Dear   :

You are in the process of transporting products for us to the following addressee:
. The shipping order for that delivery is enclosed.

We hereby direct you not to deliver said items and return them to us. We shall pay for the shipping charges. No transfer of title has occurred, nor is the customer in receipt of any bill of lading.

Sincerely,

_____

(Customer)

cc:

RETURN DEMAND

Date:

To:

Dear   :

We have been advised that your firm is insolvent. Accordingly, we demand that the products that you received from us in the past two weeks be returned to us immediately.

According to our records, you have received the following shipments from us during the past two weeks:

Sincerely,

_____

CHALLENGE TO ACCOUNT BALANCE

Date:

To:

Dear   :

Your invoice statement shows that we have an outstanding balance of
                    dollars ($). That amount is incorrect for the following
reason(s):

[ ]   The items billed have not been received.
[ ]   The account does not reflect the following payment(s):

[ ]   The account does not reflect the following credit due for returns:

[ ]   The account does not reflect credit due for damaged items.
[ ]   The prices charged are not in conformity with our contract dated
                              , 19   .

Kindly adjust our balance accordingly.

Sincerely,

_____

NOTICE: DIRECTING PAYMENT FOR NAMED ACCOUNTS

Date:

To:

Dear   :

The enclosed payment in the amount of   dollars ($)
is to be allocated to the following outstanding invoices exclusively:

Invoice Number   Amount

Sincerely,

_____

CHAPTER 7

Protecting Copyrights, Inventions, Trade Secrets and Other Intangibles

Introduction

You or your company may have certain intangible assets that far outweigh in value any fixed assets to which they attach. For example, a customer list may be a company's most valued asset. Or if your company is involved in research and development, you may assume any invention or new product that your research workers develop belongs to the company. Similarly, you may have a copyright that is far more valuable than any specific product that you sell. The forms in this chapter are designed to protect your intangible assets.

Using Your Forms

One of the most common ways to promote a product is to rely on the testimonial of a respected or well-known person. Before you can use that testimonial, you must have the person's permission. Form 701 can be used to obtain permission from an individual to use both his or her words and picture.

On occasion, you may want to use material copyrighted by someone else as part of a book you are writing or perhaps in conjunction with sales literature, or someone else may want to use your copyrighted material in his or her work. Form 702 can be used to obtain or provide such permission. Note, however, that it identifies the specific material that can be used and calls for the user to supply the original source with credit in the republication of the copyrighted material. Without that credit line, the copyright holder's right to the exclusive use of the copyrighted material may be jeopardized.

Form 703 should be used by employers to protect their ownership rights to any invention or new product that an employee creates on the employer's time, at the employer's place of business, or which is based on work performed for the employer. We suggest you have the form notarized. This will accomplish two purposes: first, it ensures that the employee knows you take this agreement very seriously; second, it will bar the employee from claiming that he or she never signed the agreement.

Form 704 should be used whenever your company receives an unsolicited idea, a proposal for a product or a product promotion. The newspapers are filled with articles reporting claims by inventors, writers, even photographers that they are owed money by companies that "used" their ideas. This form sets out the terms on which you will review the proposal. You should send two copies of the form to the person making the proposal and require a signed, notarized copy to be returned to you.

Business Tip

Avoid reading any proposal your company may receive until you receive a notarized copy of Form 704 from the person making the proposal. As soon as it becomes clear to you that a letter contains a proposal, stop reading the letter, place it in a sealed envelope and file it in your company safe or some other secure location. Immediately write a file memorandum setting out how you handled the matter. If your company receives such proposals on even a periodic basis, you may want to establish a written company policy describing how such proposals are to be handled. That policy statement should be disseminated to any employee who might receive proposals from outsiders.

Form 705 is a confidentiality agreement that you should require employees to sign if they will have access to any material that you consider secret. Such information can include, but is not limited to, customer lists, product development information, technical or manufacturing processes, pricing formulas or marketing plans. Again, we suggest that you have this form notarized, even though that step is not necessary to the enforcement of this form.

AUTHORIZATION TO USE QUOTATION

Date:

FOR GOOD AND VALUABLE CONSIDERATION, receipt of which is
acknowledged, I irrevocably grant permission to   , its
successors and assigns, to utilize the attached statement or picture in a publication
entitled   and any subsequent editions of that
publication, and in connection with the advertising or promotion of that
publication or new editions of that publication.

_____

AUTHORIZATION TO USE COPYRIGHTED MATERIALS

Date:

FOR GOOD AND VALUABLE CONSIDERATION RECEIVED, I, the owner of the copyright, authorize   to publish and reprint the following material:

This grant of permission is strictly limited to the use of the above-described material in connection with the following publication:

This grant of permission is further conditioned on the agreement of   to credit the undersigned as the author of the above-described material with a credit line that shall read as follows:

_____

INVENTION AGREEMENT BINDING EMPLOYEE

IN CONSIDERATION of being employed by
(hereinafter "Company"), I,   , intending to be legally
bound, agree as follows:

1. While employed, I will inform the Company of any inventions,
   improvements or refinements for processes or equipment that:
   (a) Came about as a result of my employment with the Company or as a
       result of any research ideas discussed between myself and any
       Company employee.
   (b) Came about while using the Company's equipment and plant, or on
       Company time or in conjunction with any Company employee.
   (c) Are related to any aspect of or line of business of the Company's
       business, either currently operating or currently being planned.
2. I hereby convey and relinquish to the Company all right and title to any of
   the inventions, improvements or refinements subject to paragraph 1 above,
   which I may create.
3. I will sign and execute any document required by the Company to
   register, perfect and protect any patent that may come about by my efforts
   on behalf of the Company.
4. This agreement shall continue in force after I have left the
   employ of the Company.

   _____

(Notary Public)

RESPONSE TO UNSOLICITED IDEAS

Date:

To:

Dear   :

Your submission of a proposal regarding   has been received by our company. As you may imagine, we receive many submissions. Your proposed submission may, in fact, already have been submitted or considered.

We will only review your proposal if you agree to the following:

1. Submissions will be returned only if you prepay shipping expenses.
2. You will not hold the company responsible for any loss or damage to any samples that you submit.
3. The company is not required to maintain confidentiality with respect to any portion of your submission.
4. The company will compensate you for your submission only if we mutually agree on all terms.

If these terms and conditions are satisfactory and you wish us to review your submission, please sign below under the words "Agreed to and accepted" and return the enclosed signed copy of this letter to us at the address shown above.

Sincerely,

_____

Agreed to and accepted:

_____

CONFIDENTIALITY AGREEMENT

FOR GOOD AND VALUABLE CONSIDERATION, receipt of which is acknowledged, and further consideration of employment with _____, I hereby acknowledge the facts set out below and agree to be bound as follows:

1. I acknowledge that during the tenure of my employment, I may come in possession of company information that the company deems to be a trade secret. Such information may be either business related (i.e., customer lists and confidential product price lists) or technically related to the company's business (i.e., engineering procedures, computer programming or research information).

2. I will not during my tenure with the company and for a period of ( ) years after I leave my employment with the company disclose to any person, company, corporation, partnership or other entity, nor use on my own, nor in conjunction with any other person, company, corporation, partnership or other entity any trade secrets of the company.

3. When my tenure of employment with the company ends, I will promptly return to the appropriate company officers all the documents of the company that are in my possession. Furthermore, I represent and warrant that I will not improperly maintain copies of any such records.

4. The company maintains the right to proceed against me for injunctive relief, should I violate the provisions of any of the above paragraphs.

5. This agreement is for the benefit of the company and shall remain in full force and effect on my heirs and successors. Furthermore, the company may transfer or assign this agreement without my consent.

_____

(Notary Public)

CHAPTER 8

Assignments

Introduction

Most business property will be sold or transferred by an assignment at one time or another. Under the laws of most states, an assignment must be in written form. This chapter will provide the forms that you will need to sell or assign virtually any form of personal property in which you own an interest. For our purposes, the term *personal property* refers to any property other than an interest in real estate.

Assigning Income and Accounts Receivable

Form 801 is a general form of assignment. When you use it, remember to fully describe the property being transferred.

Form 802 assigns income to be earned or received by the assigning party (assignor). This assignment must be given to the employer or client (if the assignor is an independent contractor) who will be paying money to the assignor.

Form 803 assigns the right to collect and receive the proceeds of a business-person's accounts receivable. If you will be the purchaser of these accounts, make sure that you are purchasing them with recourse. When you take them with recourse, you retain the right to pursue the company or person from whom you purchased the accounts in the event that you are unsuccessful in collecting on one or more of the accounts. Form 804 is an assignment without recourse. Using this form of assignment places you at greater risk (if you are buying the accounts) than if you use Form 803.

Forms 805 through 807 require both the assigning party and the receiving party to sign the agreement. Form 805 can be used when a contract is to be assigned. Form 806 should be used when a security interest is to be assigned. If you wish to assign any type of damage claim, Form 807 should be used. Form 808 is designed for use when a stock certificate will be assigned and the signature should be guaranteed by a bank or, if you are a smaller corporation, by a notary public.

If you are taking an assignment from someone who is owed a debt, make sure that you use Form 809 to notify the debtor that the amount owed will be paid to you.

Assigning Intangibles

Form 810 assigns the right to literary property for which a copyright has not been obtained. Form 811 assigns the right to copyrighted material. Form 812 can be used to assign a trademark. This assignment also should be registered with the United States Patent Office using assignment forms required by and available at the patent office.

GENERAL ASSIGNMENT

FOR GOOD AND VALUABLE CONSIDERATION, receipt of which is acknowledged, I/we hereby convey and assign to   all my/our ownership rights and interest in the following:

Dated: _____

_____

INCOME ASSIGNMENT

Date:

FOR GOOD AND VALUABLE CONSIDERATION, receipt of which is
acknowledged, I/we hereby convey and assign to
all my/our rights and interest in the proceeds and funds of a certain contract by
and between myself/ourselves and   , dated
              , 19   .

_____

_____

RECEIVABLES ASSIGNMENT

Date:

FOR GOOD AND VALUABLE CONSIDERATION, receipt of which is acknowledged, I/we hereby convey and assign to

("Assignee") all my/our ownership rights and interest in the following accounts receivables:

This transfer is made pursuant to a contract between myself/ourselves and the Assignee dated _____ , 19 __ .

I/we acknowledge that if any of the accounts transferred shall be uncollectible in part or in whole, that my/our account shall be adjusted accordingly.

_____

_____

NONRECOURSE RECEIVABLES ASSIGNMENT

Date:

FOR GOOD AND VALUABLE CONSIDERATION, receipt of which is acknowledged, I/we hereby convey and assign to

("Assignee") all my/our ownership rights and interest in the following accounts receivables:

    This transfer is made pursuant to a contract between myself/ourselves and the Assignee dated   , 19   . The Assignee acknowledges that said assignment is in satisfaction of the outstanding debt and that said transfer is without recourse for nonpayment.

_____

Assignor

_____

Assignee

CONTRACT ASSIGNMENT

FOR GOOD AND VALUABLE CONSIDERATION, receipt of which is acknowledged, I/we hereby convey and assign to
("Assignee") all my/our ownership rights and interest in the following contract:

The assignor(s) represents that the contract is assignable, that it is not for personal services and that it has not been terminated.

The Assignee shall perform all of the duties of the assignor(s) pursuant to the contract and shall indemnify the assignor(s) from any and all claims arising out of the contract.

Date:_____

_____
Assignor

_____
Assignee

SECURITY ASSIGNMENT AGREEMENT

Date:

FOR GOOD AND VALUABLE CONSIDERATION, receipt of which is acknowledged, I/we hereby convey and assign to
("Assignee") all my/our ownership rights and interest in the following security agreements:

The assignor represents that the security interest is assignable and that it has not been terminated.

The Assignee shall perform all of the duties of the assignor pursuant to the security agreement and shall indemnify the assignor from any and all claims arising out of the security agreement. Furthermore, the assignor shall provide reasonable notification to the debtor regarding this assignment.

_____
Assignor

_____
Assignee

DAMAGE CLAIM ASSIGNMENT

Date:

FOR GOOD AND VALUABLE CONSIDERATION, receipt of which is acknowledged, I/we hereby convey and assign to
("Assignee") all my/our ownership rights and interest of any type in the following claim:

The assignor represents that the claim is assignable and that it has not been settled. Furthermore, the assignor agrees to provide all reasonable assistance to the Assignee in pursuing the above-described claim.

_____
Assignor

_____
Assignee

STOCK CERTIFICATE ASSIGNMENT

Date:

FOR GOOD AND VALUABLE CONSIDERATION, receipt of which is acknowledged, I/we hereby convey and assign to _____

("Assignee") all my/our ownership rights and interest of any type whatsoever in the shares of stock of the _____ Corporation, which are represented by share certificates numbered _____ and attached hereto.

    I hereby nominate _____ as my attorney-in-fact and authorize him or her to transfer the above-described shares on the stock ledger of the above-mentioned corporation.

_____
Assignor

(Notary Public or bank verification)

NOTIFICATION OF DEBT ASSIGNMENT

Date:

To:

Dear   :

Your creditor,   , has conveyed your account to us. To guarantee that you receive proper credit, all future payments should be sent directly to us at the following address:

    Furthermore, kindly confirm that your outstanding balance is dollars ($).

Sincerely,

_____

LITERARY MATERIAL ASSIGNMENT

Date:

FOR GOOD AND VALUABLE CONSIDERATION, receipt of which is acknowledged, I/we hereby convey and assign to _____ ("Assignee") all my/our ownership rights and interest in the following literary material:

The Assignee may apply for copyrights on the material and utilize them as the owner of the same.

_____

COPYRIGHT ASSIGNMENT

Date:

FOR GOOD AND VALUABLE CONSIDERATION, receipt of which is acknowledged, I/we hereby convey and assign to _____ ("Assignee") all my/our ownership rights and interest in the following copyright:

The copyright certification is attached as Exhibit "A."

The assignor represents that he or she owns clear and marketable title to the above-described copyright and knows of no outstanding claims against the copyright.

_____

TRADEMARK ASSIGNMENT

Date:

FOR GOOD AND VALUABLE CONSIDERATION, receipt of which is
acknowledged, I/we hereby convey and assign to
("Assignee") all my/our ownership rights and interest in the following trademark:

The trademark certification is attached as Exhibit "A."

The assignor represents that he or she owns clear and marketable title to the
above-described trademark and knows of no outstanding claims against the
trademark.

_____

CHAPTER 9

Miscellaneous Forms

The forms in this chapter relate to a variety of transactions. For example, there are forms for specialized sales agreements, various types of releases and corporate transactions.

Specialized Sales and Business Agreements

Form 901 is a conditional sales agreement. In this type of transaction, the "buyer" does not actually receive title until the seller receives the last payment. Because the goods are delivered to the buyer, a stranger might well believe that the goods belong to the buyer and might either purchase them or extend credit using the goods as collateral. To avoid this, the UCC permits the seller to file a copy of the conditional sales agreement at the local filing office in the county where the goods will be located. If you are in doubt as to the proper place to file, check with your county courthouse.

Form 902 is a consignment agreement. Consigned goods are delivered to a "buyer" (the consignee) who is an agent for the seller. Nevertheless, the goods are in the "buyer's" hands and potential customers or lenders may be misled into thinking the consignee is the rightful owner of the goods. Again, the UCC protects the seller/consignor who files the consignment agreement with the proper authorities in the county in which the consignee and the goods are located.

Form 903 is an indemnification agreement that can be used for any situation in which one person agrees to indemnify the other. Note that you must identify the liability for which the indemnification is being offered. If you are to provide the indemnity, make sure that you word the description as narrowly and accurately as possible—you do not want the indemnity to go beyond what you intend to protect against. If the indemnity is being offered to you, you should be equally careful; you do not want the description to be so narrow that it does not include matters that cause you concern.

Form 904 is the stock purchase agreement that you can use when your corporation sells shares of its stock to a new investor.

Form 905 is the noncompetition agreement that can be used if your business relies on independent contractors who must be given access to company secrets. The noncompetition contract set out in Chapter 5 should be used when you hire an employee; Form 905 should be used for independent contractors. Do not assume that this agreement should be used only for high-level consultants. If, for example, you use a local person to keyboard and print your customer mailing list, that person will have complete access to your most precious business asset.

Form 906 can be used to transfer title to virtually any type of personal property. It contains the seller's representations of good title and warranties by both parties that the sale was not effected through a broker.

Specialized Contract Forms

Forms 907 and 908 extend the time to complete an agreement. Form 907 can be used if the contract is being extended; Form 908 can be used to allow one party more time to complete his or her end of the bargain.

Form 909 should be used when both parties agree to end an existing contractual relationship. Prudent businesspeople generally use a witness (or notary) to ensure that the signing is not questioned at some later date.

Forms 910 through 912 offer release formats. Although not required by law, it is prudent to have a third person (or a notary public) witness the signing of the release forms.

Form 910 is a general release in which one person releases the other from liability. It can be used for any type of liability. In Form 911 both sides release the other. Form 912 can be used to issue a release of a mechanic's or materialman's lien against real property.

Corporate and Partnership Forms

Forms 913 and 914 are proxy forms designed to be used when one person agrees to let another person vote the first person's corporate stock. These forms can be used in conjunction with a loan (e.g., where the shares are pledged as collateral) or in conjunction with the sale of the shares after the record date and before a shareholders' meeting.

Neither of these forms should be used if the corporation's board of directors issues the proxy. In such cases, you must seek out your company's attorney before issuing a proxy. Form 913 is a simple, straightforward revocable proxy. Under state law, it can be revoked at any time. The person granting the proxy need only attend the meeting and announce that he or she is revoking the proxy and will vote the shares himself or herself. Form 914 is irrevocable. This means the proxy may not be rescinded during the term noted on the proxy.

Form 915 can be used to create a partnership form of business. Once you and your partner have agreed on the amounts that each of you will invest in the business and how each of you will share in its profits, you have all the information you need to complete this form.

Powers of Attorney

Forms 916 and 917 are powers of attorney. Most people think of powers of attorney in the context of incompetent persons. However, they also have their place in the small business setting. If, for example, you operate a small business and expect to be absent because you will be taking that long-awaited extended vacation, you may have to delegate specific authority to a trusted individual. People accustomed to dealing directly with you may not be willing to deal with a subordinate in the absence of some form of written authorization.

Form 916 sets out a power of attorney for a limited purpose—you must describe the power you are granting precisely to ensure that your representative can do everything you wish him or her to do, but no more than that. Form 917 is a general, unlimited power of attorney. Both forms must be notarized.

Affidavits and Bulk Sales

Forms 918 and 919 are required to comply with the Bulk Sales provisions of the UCC. A bulk sale is one that you would not make in the ordinary course of business. For example, if you operated a shop that offered duplicating services, you would not, as part of your ordinary business operations, sell your duplicating machines and your entire stock of toner and paper.

Forms 918 and 919 should be used only if your existing creditors can be paid in full from the sale proceeds. If not, consult with your attorney before going ahead with the sale.

Form 918 provides the affidavit required for a bulk sale. This form must be notarized. Form 919 provides creditors with notice of the sale. You must give creditors at least ten days' notice of the scheduled sale date. Although not required by law, hand delivery with an affidavit that delivery was made, or registered mail, return receipt requested, are the recommended forms of service.

CONDITIONAL SALE AGREEMENT

AGREEMENT made this   day of   , 19   , by and between
                                    (hereinafter "Seller") and
(hereinafter "Buyer").

    Intending to be legally bound, the Buyer and the Seller agree as follows:

1. The Seller will sell to the Buyer and the Buyer will purchase the items listed on Schedule A.

2. The purchase price shall be:
   Price: Sales tax: Finance charges:
   Shipping charges: Total price:

3. The purchase price shall be paid with a down payment of
   dollars ($) and the remaining amount in equal installments of
              dollars ($), payable on the   day of the
   month.

4. This is a conditional sales agreement. Title will not pass to the Buyer until payment in full has been received by the Seller.

5. The Seller retains the right to repossess the items sold, subject to any apportionment for payments received, should the Buyer fail or refuse to make all necessary payments.

_____
Buyer

_____
Seller

THIS FORM MUST BE RECORDED WITH YOUR LOCAL FILING OFFICE
OR IT WILL NOT BE EFFECTIVE AGAINST SUBSEQUENT LENDERS.

CONSIGNMENT AGREEMENT

THIS CONSIGNMENT AGREEMENT is made this   day of   ,
19   , by and between   (hereinafter "Consignor") and
                              (hereinafter "Consignee").

The parties intending to be legally bound agree as follows:

1. The property delivered to the Consignee, as listed in the attached
    schedule, shall remain the property of the Consignor.
2. The Consignee will display the items delivered at its business location.
3. The Consignee will return on demand any property of the Consignor prior
    to its sale, and the Consignee promises to return said property in good and
    marketable condition.
4. The Consignee will use its best business efforts to sell said items on
    behalf of the Consignor, at a minimum price as established by the
    Consignor.
5. The Consignee will remit the proceeds of the sale to the Consignor
    within   (   ) days of sale, said funds to be segregated from the
    accounts of the Consignee.
6. The Consignee will permit and allow the Consignor to inspect and audit
    the books and records of the Consignee with respect to the property of the
    Consignor.
7. The Consignee will execute all reasonable documents necessary to protect
    and ensure that the title to the items remains with the Consignor.

_____
Consignee

_____ _____
Consignor

THIS FORM MUST BE RECORDED WITH YOUR LOCAL FILING OFFICE
OR IT WILL NOT BE EFFECTIVE AGAINST SUBSEQUENT LENDERS.

INDEMNIFICATION AGREEMENT

IN CONSIDERATION OF GOOD AND VALUABLE CONSIDERATION, by this agreement made this   day of   , 19   , between   (the "Seller") and   (the "Purchaser"), the parties hereby agree:

1. <u>Indemnification.</u> The Seller agrees to indemnify and hold the Purchaser harmless at all times against and in respect of all actions, claims, suits, settlements, proceedings, demands, assessments, judgments, losses, costs, damages, disbursements and expenses incident to, arising from or with respect to the following transaction:

2. <u>Notice.</u> The Purchaser shall notify the Seller within   (   ) days after receipt by the Purchaser of any notice of any information referable to Paragraph 1 above. However, the omission to so notify the Seller shall not relieve the Seller of any obligation on account thereof, except to the extent that the Seller was prejudiced by the Purchaser's failure to provide such notice.

3. <u>Benefit.</u> This agreement shall be binding upon and inure to the benefit of the parties hereto and their legal representatives, successors and assigns.

4. <u>Interpretation.</u> This agreement shall be interpreted in accordance with the laws of the state of   .

5. <u>Invalid Provision.</u> In the event any provision of this agreement is held to be void, invalid or unenforceable in any respect, then the same shall not affect the remaining provisions hereof, which shall continue in full force and effect.

6. <u>Entire Agreement.</u> This agreement contains the entire understanding of the parties. It may not be changed orally. This agreement may be amended or

modified only in writing and such writing must be executed by both parties hereto.

IN WITNESS WHEREOF, the parties have executed this agreement the day and year first above written.

_____
Purchaser

_____
Seller

(Notary Public)

SUBSCRIPTION TO CORPORATE STOCK

FOR VALUABLE CONSIDERATION RECEIVED, I agree to purchase
(   ) shares of the capital stock of   (hereinafter
"Corporation") at a price of   dollars ($) per share for a
total amount of   dollars ($).

    I have been informed that the shares I am purchasing will have all of the
rights and privileges of all shares of the same class of stock. Furthermore, I am
aware that the shares I am purchasing equal   percent (%) of all issued
and outstanding stock of the same class and percent   (%) of all of the
issued and outstanding stock of the corporation, regardless of class.

    The purchase price will be paid to the Corporation on or before
       , 19   .

_____
Purchaser

Agreed to and accepted:

_____
For the Above-Mentioned Corporation

NONCOMPETITION AGREEMENT

FOR CONSIDERATION RECEIVED, this agreement made this   day of
                , 19   , by and between   (hereinafter
referred to as the "Principal") and   (hereinafter referred
to as the "Consultant").

WHEREAS, the Principal desires to engage the services of the Consultant to
assist the Principal in the operation of its business, it is agreed as follows:

1. Purpose. The Principal engages the Consultant to assist the Principal in the
   operation of its business.

2. Term. This agreement shall commence on   , 19   ,
   and shall terminate on   , 19   .

3. Disclosure of Information. The Consultant acknowledges that the list of
   the Principal's customers as it may exist from time to time is a valuable,
   special and unique asset of the Principal's business. The Consultant shall
   not, during or after the term of this agreement, disclose the list of the
   Principal's customers or any part thereof to any person, firm, corporation,
   association or other entity for any reason or purpose whatsoever. In the
   event of a breach or threatened breach by the Consultant of the provisions
   of this paragraph, the Principal shall be entitled to an injunction
   restraining the Consultant from disclosing, in whole or in part, the list of
   the Principal's customers or from rendering any services to any person,
   firm, corporation, association or other entity to whom such list, in whole
   or in part, has been disclosed or is threatened to be disclosed. Nothing
   herein shall be construed as prohibiting the Principal from pursuing any
   other remedies available to the Principal for such breach or threatened
   breach, including the recovery of damages from the Consultant.

4. Notices. Any notice required or desired to be given under this agreement
   shall be deemed given if in writing sent by certified mail to his or her
   residence in the case of the Consultant or to its principal office in the case
   of the Principal.

5. Assignment. The Consultant acknowledges that the services to be rendered
   by him or her are unique and personal. Accordingly, the Consultant may
   not assign any of his or her rights or delegate any of his or her duties or

obligations under this agreement. The rights and obligations of the Principal under this agreement shall inure to the benefit of and shall be binding upon the successors and assigns of the Principal.

6. <u>Status of Consultant.</u> The Consultant is engaged as an independent contractor and shall be treated as such for all purposes, including, but not limited to, federal and state taxation, withholding, unemployment insurance and workers' compensation. The Consultant will not be considered an employee for any purpose.

7. <u>Entire Agreement.</u> This agreement contains the entire understanding of the parties. It may not be changed orally but only by an agreement in writing signed by the party against whom enforcement of any waiver, change, modification, extension or discharge is sought.

IN WITNESS WHEREOF, the parties have executed this agreement the day and year first above written.

_____
Principal

_____
Consultant

WITNESS:

_____

PERSONAL PROPERTY SALES CONTRACT

AGREEMENT made this   day of   , 19   , between
                (hereinafter "Seller") and
(hereinafter "Purchaser").

1. <u>The Property.</u> The Seller has agreed to sell and the Purchaser has agreed to buy the following personal property:

2. <u>Purchase Price.</u> The purchase price for the property described in paragraph 1 above shall be   dollars ($) and shall be paid as follows:

    (a)   dollars ($) upon the execution of this agreement and

    (b) The balance of   dollars ($) payable in (   ) equal monthly installments with interest at the rate of   percent   (%) per annum, the first payment to begin (   ) days after the execution of this agreement. This obligation shall be evidenced by a promissory note, a copy being attached hereto, made a part hereof and designated as "Exhibit A."

3. <u>Warranties of the Seller.</u> The Seller hereby warrants and represents to the Purchaser that:

    (a) The Seller owns and has good and marketable title to the property being conveyed herein, free and clear of any pledges, liens, judgments, encumbrances, security interests, claims or contract rights, and further promises and covenants to refrain from so encumbering same from the date of execution of this agreement until closing;

    (b) No approval or consent of any third person is required to effect the sale;

    (c) The execution and performance of this agreement will not violate any agreements to which the Seller is a party or any federal, state or local laws, rules or regulations;

    (d) The Seller's representations, warranties and agreements shall be true and complete as of the date hereof and as of the closing and shall survive the closing and the transactions contemplated by this agreement.

4. Broker. Both the Seller and the Purchaser warrant and represent that no broker was involved in negotiating this purchase and sale, and both the Seller and the Purchaser agree to indemnify and hold each other harmless against any and all claims for brokerage.

5. Benefit. This agreement shall be binding upon and inure to the benefit of the parties hereto and their legal representatives, successors and assigns.

6. Interpretation. This agreement shall be interpreted in accordance with the laws of the state of   .

7. Invalid Provision. In the event any provision or subprovision of this agreement is held to be void, invalid or unenforceable in any respect, then the same shall not affect the remaining provisions or subprovisions hereof, which shall continue in full force and effect.

8. Entire Agreement. This agreement contains the entire understanding of the parties. It may not be changed orally. This agreement may only be amended or modified in writing and with such writing being executed by both parties hereto.

IN WITNESS WHEREOF, the parties have executed this agreement the day and year first above written.

_____
Seller

_____
Purchaser

WITNESS:

_____

AGREEMENT EXTENDING A CONTRACT

FOR CONSIDERATION mutually exchanged between the parties,

               and   , this extension
agreement is made this   day of   , 19   .

     WHEREAS,   and
have previously entered into an agreement dated   , 19   ,
and

     WHEREAS, said agreement will conclude on   , 19   ,
and

     WHEREAS, both parties desire to extend the above-mentioned agreement,

NOW, therefore, intending to be legally bound, both parties agree as follows:

1. The agreement shall be lengthened for an additional term of

2. In all other respects, said agreement shall continue in full force and effect.

     IN WITNESS WHEREOF, the parties have executed this agreement the day
and year first above written.

                          _____

                          _____

WITNESS:

_____

PERFORMANCE EXTENSION

FOR CONSIDERATION mutually exchanged between the parties,
                    and   , this performance
extension agreement is made this   day of   , 19   .

    WHEREAS,   and   have
previously entered into an agreement dated   , 19   , and

    WHEREAS, said agreement requires performance on or before   ,
19   ,

    WHEREAS, both parties desire to extend the agreement,

    NOW, therefore, intending to be legally bound, both parties agree as follows:

1. The due date of performance shall be   , 19   .

2. In all other respects, said agreement shall continue in full force and effect.

    IN WITNESS WHEREOF, the parties have executed this agreement the day
and year first above written.

                                         _____

                                       _____

WITNESS:

_____

CONTRACT TERMINATION

FOR CONSIDERATION mutually exchanged between the parties,
        and   , this agreement is made this
    day of   , 19   .

    WHEREAS,   and   have
previously entered into an agreement dated   , 19   ; and

    WHEREAS, both parties desire to terminate the agreement:

    NOW, therefore intending to be legally bound, both parties agree as follows:

1. The above-described agreement shall cease as of   ,
   19   .

2. Both parties agree to release each other of liability.

3. In all other respects, said agreement shall continue in full force and effect.

    IN WITNESS WHEREOF, the parties have executed this agreement the day and year first above written.

_____

_____

WITNESS:

_____

GENERAL RELEASE

Date:

IN CONSIDERATION of one dollar ($1) and other valuable consideration received, I,   , relieve and release
(hereinafter "Obligor"), his or her heirs and assigns from all claims and liabilities owed to me by the Obligor as of the date of the execution of this release.

_____

(Notary Public)

MUTUAL RELEASE

Date:

IN CONSIDERATION of one dollar ($1), this mutual release and other valuable consideration received,   and
relieve, release and discharge each other, their heirs and assigns from all claims and liabilities or obligations whether flowing from contracts, lawsuits or any other source and that will have arisen on or before the date of this release.

_____

_____

(Notary Public)

LIEN RELEASE

IN CONSIDERATION of one dollar ($1) and other valuable consideration received, I, _____ , relieve and release from all mechanics, materialman or labor liens that I have filed, before the date set out below, against the real property located at:

Date: _____

_____

(Notary Public)

REVOCABLE PROXY

FOR AND IN CONSIDERATION of one dollar ($1) and other valuable consideration, I hereby bestow on a proxy to vote on my behalf   (   ) shares of   (hereinafter "Corporation") at the shareholders' meeting to be held on   , 19   , and all subsequent regular and special meetings of shareholders of the Corporation.

   The holder of this proxy shall have all the rights and privileges to vote and attend meetings as I do. Until this proxy is revoked, I shall not act to vote the shares represented by this proxy. This proxy is revocable without notice.

Date: _____

_____

IRREVOCABLE PROXY

FOR AND IN CONSIDERATION of one dollar ($1), I hereby bestow on
_____ a proxy to vote on my behalf   (   ) shares of
stock of _____ (hereinafter "Company") at the shareholders'
meeting to be held on _____ , 19   .

    The holder of this proxy shall have all the rights and privileges to vote and
attend the aforesaid meeting as I do. This proxy, which may not be revoked by me,
shall not extend beyond the shareholders' meeting, or any extension thereof, to be
held on _____ , 19   .

Date: _____

                                                 _____

PARTNERSHIP AGREEMENT

THIS AGREEMENT made this   day of   , 19   , by and among   (hereinafter referred to as "Partner One") and (hereinafter referred to as "Partner Two").

WHEREAS, Partner One and Partner Two desire to form a partnership in the state of   .

NOW, THEREFORE, in consideration of the mutual covenants and agreements contained herein, the parties hereto, intending to be legally bound hereby, agree as follows:

1. The parties hereby form a partnership that will engage in the business of   under the name of   .

2. The partners ownership interest and capital account shall be as follows:

3. The principal office of the partnership is to be located at   , or in such other place as the parties may agree.

4. The partnership shall exist for a period of   , commencing on   , 19   , and shall continue until   , 19   , unless terminated earlier as hereinafter provided.

5. Either party to this partnership agreement may withdraw from the partnership upon six (6) months' notice to the remaining party to this partnership agreement.

6. The partners shall share the profits and losses of the partnership in relationship to their ownership interest.

7. This partnership agreement shall immediately terminate upon the death of either partner.

8. All controversies arising under or in connection with, or relating to any alleged breach of, this partnership agreement shall be settled by

arbitration in accordance with the rules then obtaining of the American Arbitration Association, and judgment upon any award rendered may be entered in any court having jurisdiction.

9. This partnership agreement shall be binding upon and inure to the benefit of the parties hereto and their respective heirs, executors, administrators, successors and assigns.

10. This partnership agreement constitutes the entire agreement between the parties hereto and supersedes all prior agreements, negotiations and understandings of any nature with respect to the subject matter hereto. No amendment, waiver or discharge of any of the provisions of this agreement shall be effective against any party unless that party shall have consented thereto in writing.

11. This partnership agreement shall be construed, interpreted and enforced in accordance with the laws of the state of _____ .

IN WITNESS WHEREOF, Partner One and Partner Two have caused this partnership agreement to be duly executed the day and year set out above.

IN WITNESS WHEREOF, the parties have executed this agreement the day and year first above written.

_____

_____

WITNESS: _____

LIMITED POWER OF ATTORNEY

KNOW ALL PERSONS BY THESE PRESENTS, that I,
                    , residing at   , do
hereby make, constitute and appoint   , residing at
                    , as the true and lawful attorney-in-fact for me
and in my name, place and stead, and on my behalf, and for my use and benefit
with respect to the following matter(s):

    This instrument shall be construed and interpreted as a limited power of
attorney.

    The enumeration of specific items, rights or powers herein shall not limit or
restrict, and is not to be construed or interpreted as limiting or restricting, the
limited powers herein granted to said attorney-in-fact.

    The rights, powers and authority of said attorney-in-fact granted in this
instrument shall commence and be in full force and effect on
, 19   , and such rights, powers and authority shall remain in full force and effect
thereafter until I,   , give notice in writing that such
power is terminated.

    It is my desire, and I so freely state, that this power of attorney shall not be
affected by my subsequent disability or incapacity. Furthermore, upon a finding of
incompetence by a court of appropriate jurisdiction, this power of attorney shall
be irrevocable until such time as said court determines that I am no longer
incompetent.

_____

    I,   , whose name is signed to the foregoing
instrument, having been duly qualified according to the law, do hereby
acknowledge that I signed and executed this power of attorney; that I am of sound
mind; that I am eighteen (18) years of age or older; that I signed it willingly and
am under no constraint or undue influence; and that I signed it as my free and
voluntary act for the purpose therein expressed.

_____

(Notary Public)

FULL POWER OF ATTORNEY

Date:

KNOW ALL PERSONS BY THESE PRESENTS, that I,

, residing at   , do
hereby make, constitute and appoint   , residing at
                          , as the true and lawful attorney-in-fact for me
and in my name, place and stead, and on my behalf, and for my use and benefit, in
the following matters:

1. To ask, demand, sue for, recover and receive all manner of goods, chattels, debts, rents, interest, sums of money and demands whatsoever, due or hereafter to become due and owing, or belonging to me, and to make, give and execute acquittances, receipts, satisfactions or other discharges for the same, whether under seal or otherwise;

2. To make, execute, endorse, accept and deliver in my name or in the name of my aforesaid attorney all checks, notes, drafts, warrants, acknowledgments, agreements and all other instruments in writing, of whatever nature, as to my said attorney-in-fact may seem necessary to conserve my interests;

3. To execute, acknowledge and deliver any and all contracts, debts, leases, assignments of mortgage, extensions of mortgage, satisfactions of mortgage, releases of mortgage, subordination agreements and any other instrument or agreement of any kind or nature whatsoever, in connection therewith, and affecting any and all property presently mine or hereafter acquired, located anywhere, which to my said attorney-in-fact may seem necessary or advantageous for my interests;

4. To enter into and take possession of any lands, real estate, tenements, houses, stores or buildings, or parts thereof, belonging to me that may become vacant or unoccupied, or to the possession of which I may be or may become entitled, and to receive and take for me and in my name and to my use all or any rents, profits or issues of any real estate to me belonging, and to let the same in such manner as to my attorney shall seem necessary and proper, and from time to time to renew leases;

5. To commence and prosecute in my behalf any suits or actions or other legal or equitable proceedings for the recovery of any of my lands or for any goods, chattels, debts, duties, demand, cause or thing whatsoever, due or to become due or belonging to me, and to prosecute, maintain and discontinue the same, if he or she shall deem proper;

6. To take all steps and remedies necessary and proper for the conduct and management of my business affairs, and for the recovery, receiving, obtaining and holding possession of any lands, tenements, rents or real estate, goods and chattels, debts, interest, demands, duties, sum or sums of money or any other thing whatsoever, located anywhere, that is, are or shall be, by my said attorney-in-fact, thought to be due, owing, belonging to or payable to me in my own right or otherwise;

7. To appear, answer and defend in all actions and suits whatsoever that shall be commenced against me and also for me and in my name to compromise, settle and adjust, with each and every person or persons, all actions, accounts, dues and demands, subsisting or to subsist between me and them or any of them, and in such manner as my said attorney-in-fact shall think proper; hereby giving to my said attorney power and authority to do, execute and perform and finish for me and in my name all those things that shall be expedient and necessary, or which my said attorney shall judge expedient and necessary in and about or concerning the premises, or any of them, as fully as I could do if personally present, hereby ratifying and confirming whatever my said attorney shall do or cause to be done in, about or concerning the premises and any part thereof.

This instrument shall be construed and interpreted as a general power of attorney.

The enumeration of specific items, rights or powers herein shall not limit or restrict, and is not to be construed or interpreted as limiting or restricting, the general powers herein granted to said attorney-in-fact.

The rights, powers and authority of said attorney-in-fact granted in this instrument shall commence and be in full force and effect on   ,
19   , and such rights, powers and authority shall remain in full force and effect thereafter until I give notice in writing that such power is terminated.

It is my desire, and I so freely state, that this power of attorney shall not be affected by my subsequent disability or incapacity. Furthermore, upon a finding of incompetence by a court of appropriate jurisdiction, this power of attorney shall be irrevocable until such time as said court determines that I am no longer incompetent.

_____

I,   , whose name is signed to the foregoing instrument, having been duly qualified according to the law, do hereby acknowledge that I signed and executed this power of attorney; that I am of sound mind; that I am eighteen (18) years of age or older; that I signed it willingly and am under no constraint or undue influence; and that I signed it as my free and voluntary act for the purpose therein expressed.

_____

(Notary Public)

BULK SALES AFFIDAVIT

State of   :

County of   :

The undersigned,   , residing at

        , being duly sworn, deposes:

1. I am the   President and sole shareholder of the
   business known as   (hereinafter
   "Corporation") and I am the person who executed the annexed bill of sale
   on behalf of the Corporation.

2. The Corporation is the sole owner of the property described in the
   foregoing bill of sale, and it has the full right to sell and transfer this
   property.

3. All of the property described in the foregoing bill of sale is free and clear
   of all obligations and encumbrances.

4. There are no judgments existing against the Corporation in any court; nor
   are there any replevins, liens, attachments or executions issued against the
   Corporation; nor has any petition in bankruptcy nor any arrangement
   proceeding been filed by or against the Corporation; nor has the
   Corporation taken advantage of any law relating to insolvency.

This affidavit is made to induce   (hereinafter
"Buyer") to accept the transfer of the property described in the foregoing bill of
sale and to pay consideration therefor. It also is made to assure compliance with
the bulk transfer provisions of the Uniform Commercial Code as it is in force in
the state of   and to assure that there are no creditors of the
Corporation who are entitled to the statutory notice of sale.

_____

(Notary Public)

Index

About the Author

Ted Nicholas is a multifaceted business personality. In addition to being a well-known author and respected speaker, Mr. Nicholas remains an active participant in his own entrepreneurial ventures. Without capital, he started his first business at age 21. Since then, he has started 22 companies of his own.

Mr. Nicholas has written 13 books on business and finance since his writing career began in 1972. The best known is *How To Form Your Own Corporation Without a Lawyer for under $75*. His previous business enterprises include Enterprise Publishing, Inc., The Company Corporation and Peterson's House of Fudge, a candy and ice cream manufacturing business conducted through 30 retail stores, as well as other businesses in franchising, real estate, machinery and food.

When the author was only 29, he was selected by a group of business leaders as one of the most outstanding businessmen in the nation and was invited to the White House to meet the President.

Although Mr. Nicholas has founded many successful enterprises, he also has experienced two major setbacks and many minor ones. He considers business setbacks necessary to success and the only true way to learn anything in life, a lesson that goes all the way back to childhood. That's why he teaches other entrepreneurs how to "fail forward."

Mr. Nicholas has appeared on numerous television and radio shows and conducts business seminars in Florida, Switzerland, the UK, Germany and France. Presently, he owns and operates four corporations of his own and acts as marketing consultant and copywriter to small as well as large businesses.

If you have any questions, thoughts or comments, Mr. Nicholas loves to hear from his readers! You are welcome to call, write or fax him at

P.O. Box 877
Indian Rocks Beach, FL 34635
Phone: 813-596-4966
Fax: 813-596-6900

LICENSE AGREEMENT

OPENING ENVELOPE VOIDS RETURNABILITY OR MONEY-BACK GUARANTEES
PLEASE READ THIS DOCUMENT CAREFULLY BEFORE BREAKING THIS SEAL

SOFTWARE REGISTRATION

Congratulations on the purchase of your new **Business Agreements Kit** book/disk package. Please complete this form, tear it out, fold, tape and mail it back to us so our software support department will know who you are, should you need to call in for help.

Name _____

Title _____

Company _____

Address _____

City _____ State _____

Zip Code _____

Day Telephone (   ) _____

Fax (   ) _____

Please rate the following products on how useful you would find them in running your business:

1. A small business legal guide that helps you understand legal issues, describes how to protect your assets and provides ready-to-use forms.
 ○ Not at all useful ○ Somewhat useful ○ Very useful

2. A collection of corporate forms to help you keep internal records to prevent lawsuits from piercing the corporate veil.
 ○ Not at all useful ○ Somewhat useful ○ Very useful

3. A hands-on guide for showing you how and why to write a business plan.
 ○ Not at all useful ○ Somewhat useful ○ Very useful

4. What type of computer do you own?
 ○ IBM or IBM-Compatible ○ 3½" disk ○ 5¼" disk
 ○ Macintosh   ○ Other

5. Does your computer have a CD-ROM drive?
 ○ Yes ○ No

6. Please tell us about the biggest challenges you face in operating your business.

_____

_____

_____

_____

UPSTART

The Small Business Publishing Company
a division of Dearborn Publishing Group, Inc.
155 North Wacker Drive
Chicago, IL 60606-1719
Software Support: 1-312-836-4400 extension 3400
Hours: Monday – Friday, 9 a.m. – 5 p.m., C.S.T.

IMPORTANT—PLEASE FOLD OVER—PLEASE TAPE BEFORE MAILING

Return Address:

||||||

First Class
U.S. Postage
PAID
Dearborn Financial
Publishing, Inc.

BUSINESS REPLY MAIL
FIRST CLASS MAIL PERMIT NO. 88177 CHICAGO, IL

POSTAGE WILL BE PAID BY ADDRESSEE:

UPSTART

Software Registration
155 North Wacker Drive
Chicago, Illinois 60606-9545

IMPORTANT—PLEASE FOLD OVER—PLEASE TAPE BEFORE MAILING

NOTE: This page, when folded over and taped, becomes an
envelope, which has been approved by the United States
Postal Service. It is provided for your convenience.